The *Secret Identity* of Chance

The True Story of a Father and Adopted Daughter Miraculously Brought Together after Forty Years

Marla McKeown

The Secret Identity of Chance
Trilogy Christian Publishers A Wholly Owned Subsidiary of Trinity Broadcasting Network
2442 Michelle Drive Tustin, CA 92780
Copyright © 2023 by Marla Sue Higgins

No part of this book may be reproduced, stored in a retrieval system, or transmitted by any means without written permission from the author. All rights reserved. Printed in the USA.

Rights Department, 2442 Michelle Drive, Tustin, CA 92780.

Trilogy Christian Publishing/TBN and colophon are trademarks of Trinity Broadcasting Network.

For information about special discounts for bulk purchases, please contact Trilogy Christian Publishing.

Trilogy Disclaimer: The views and content expressed in this book are those of the author and may not necessarily reflect the views and doctrine of Trilogy Christian Publishing or the Trinity Broadcasting Network.

10 9 8 7 6 5 4 3 2 1

Library of Congress Cataloging-in-Publication Data is available.

ISBN: 979-8-89041-408-3

E-ISBN: 979-8-89041-409-0

Dedication

Affectionately dedicated to my daughters, Paris Elisé Louise and Chanel Bellina. You are the loves of my life, and you will always be my "why."

This book is also dedicated to my father, John Stuart McKeown, an extraordinary man. There is not another like you; we were chosen for each other, and your legacy lives on. And to my biological mother, Shirlee Ann, for your bravery and sacrificial love, without which I wouldn't be here.

Acknowledgments

I wish to express my deepest appreciation . . .

To Miss Dodie: Your passionate encouragement for me to tell my story was a gift. I opened it with care, and I'm grateful for your belief in me early on, even when I struggled to see it myself.

To my dearest Carrin: Thank you for the endless hours, late into the night, when you allowed me to read you page after page, and through my struggle to find my own voice, you constantly challenged me to go deeper, as you shouted from the Flight Tower, "Land the plane, Marla Sue, land the plane!" You were my guiding light.

To both my adoptive and biological families: I am equal parts of both of you. I'm grateful for the role you have each played in my life, and how it has allowed me to find unique ways of looking at the world from many different points of view. I deeply love and respect the uniqueness of my relationships with all of you. I appreciate your encouragement and support as you entrusted me to tell a bit of "our story."

To Mike Valentine: There is no power like that of a good editor! Thank you.

To every person who has had a difficult or painful story and found the courage to share it with the world: Your story matters, and I applaud you.

To the God I love, who held my hand throughout this journey, and never let go.

Contents

1. A Fighting Chance 7
2. Second Chance 11
3. Chance Remembrance 19
4. Leave to Chance. 23
5. Take a Chance 29
6. One Chance in a Million 37
7. Slim Chance 57
8. Second Chance 63
9. Jump at the Chance 75
10. A Chance Meeting 87
11. Chance of a Lifetime 113
12. Not a Chance in Hell 131

Chapter 1

A Fighting Chance

The Lady with the Lamp

*Lo! In that house of misery, A lady with a lamp I see,
Pass through the glimmering gloom, And flit from
room to room.*

—Henry Wadsworth Longfellow

The founding angel of modern nursing:
Florence Nightingale

When I was born in 1963, Rose was a medical missionary nurse working at Sutter Memorial Hospital. She was on sabbatical from the medical missionary work she normally did abroad. Rose was my pseudo "Florence Nightingale." The specialized environment of the neonatal intensive care unit (NICU) is demanding, both physically and psychologically. Not every baby makes it, even after weeks and months of intensive care. She was my lifeline during the first minutes, hours, days, and weeks of my life. Rose was not just a source of love and nurturing during the crucial development stages of my growth, but she was also directly responsible for finding the people I would eventually call "my parents." She changed the trajectory of my life.

The Secret Identity of Chance

Rose was acquainted with my parents through their church affiliation and was keenly aware of their desperation to adopt a baby girl. Soon after I was born, she called them to say, "We have a preemie baby girl who was just born, and she needs a good home." During the monthlong duration of my hospital stay, the process of finding a parental match started immediately. The adoption process can be expensive, arduous, emotional, and stressful. When you commit to adoption, there is so much on the line. Although there are currently about 1.5 million adopted children in the United States—2 percent of the population, or one out of every fifty children—I never met another person outside of my immediate family who was adopted, with the exception of my younger brother, Kevin. Although we came from different biological families, the subject always felt strictly taboo. There was never a word about adoption spoken between us growing up, and it wasn't until we were well into our adult years that we finally opened up.

Mine was a "secret adoption," meaning the record of my biological parent(s) was protected under a sealed court order, and rarely would the name of the biological father even be recorded. Upon my release from the hospital, I was issued a new birth certificate with the names of my adoptive parents, and my new given name: Marla Sue.

You can ignore your heart and mind, but it will always find its way home.

—Shannon L. Alder

Outwardly, everything seemed in order, but I still wrestled with what parts of me were born out of my environment, and what parts of me were innate, originating from my DNA. Something always drew me back to the place where it all began, but it was a mystery, and one that nobody could solve for me.

Chapter 1: A Fighting Chance

The science behind animals that find their way back home over long distances has always fascinated me. Somehow, without maps, GPS, or "Siri," their powerful innate instincts drive them, giving them the ability to find their way home. I read a story years ago where a dog was taken from its owner to a new location hundreds of miles by car, and yet it found its way back home on foot! There was no "route" or scent to follow; the dog made its way by pure instinct. It seems impossible, but the reality is that deep within the heart of all creation is an unquenchable desire to connect with our providential place of origin. We will go to the ends of the earth, risk unimaginable perils, even fight until our last breath, just to be united with those to whom we belong.

It's a delicate and beautiful thread that weaves itself throughout humanity, as well as the animal kingdom. We are clearly hardwired to connect with our origins. When that vital link has been disrupted or severed, the innate intuitive nature of our very being longs to draw us back. Being adopted forced me to disengage with a part of myself, a part that felt exiled by the loss of a lineage and cultural identity I would never know.

I'm not sure exactly when the decision was made that I would not go home with my birth mother (or why), but my fate was sealed that day. The woman who gave me life was leaving the hospital without me. Although times have changed considerably since 1963, it was believed at that time that adoptive mothers could not adequately bond with their babies unless the babies were taken away from the biological mother immediately after birth. As unbearable as it was, women who planned on giving up their babies for adoption were prevented from seeing them. The opinion was that infants would bond more successfully with their adoptive families if they were placed with them as soon as possible, and the biological mothers were expected to "forget about their child and get on with their lives."

The anguished wails of a young woman walking out of the hospital being held up by her mother caught the attention of my parents as they crossed paths, the day they came to pick me up from the hospital. Even amidst the excitement and details of that day, my mom never forgot the brokenhearted faces of those two women. The younger woman was a beautiful blonde, about the same age as my adoptive mother would have been at the time. The older woman was no doubt her mother. The incident resonated with my parents for days thereafter, until it dawned on them: those two women were quite possibly my birth mother and grandmother. Could it have been possible that my birth mother came that day to say her final good-byes? And would these strangers ever reappear in my life again? Whatever my identity was, or would have been, it had now been filed away under a court order, and all that remained of my genesis lay dormant within me. However, most things that are buried will eventually find their way to the top.

Chapter 2

Second Chance

Every new beginning comes from some other beginning's end.

—Seneca

The social unrest in Sacramento during the 1960s left my parents yearning for small-town life as a way to raise their family. They had hopes of finding such a place in Southern California, and so they packed up and made the trek to sunny Orange County. I was almost three when we moved into our little house on Killarney Road; it was the only place that ever really felt like home. The pace of life was slow, and small-town communities grew close. There was a sweet sense of safety and security in the world around me. It was a little slice of the "American dream" for my parents, who bought their modest 1,300-square-foot, four-bedroom house on the corner of Killarney and Monroe Avenue. Luscious night-blooming jasmine bushes lined the perimeter of our little house, with its sweet, intoxicating fragrance so potent that when the summer breeze blew just right, you could smell it blocks away.

Our house was perfectly situated between boundless Valencia orange groves and succulent strawberry fields, which blanketed the county for miles in every direction. Thanks to ubiquitous sprawling dairy farms, we had fresh, cold milk delivered (in large, glass quart-sized mason jars) to our front doorstep every other morning by our friendly neighborhood "milkman." Neighbors rarely locked their front doors at night, and kids spent warm summer days by the pool or riding bikes through miles of orange groves. Kids were instructed to be home "before the streetlights turned on," while the Disneyland fireworks went off promptly at 9:30 p.m. without fail. This quaint and picturesque little farmland community became the cherished place I called home. It was host to many colorful characters and a treasure trove of childhood memories and lifelong friendships. It had all the charm and simplicity of "small town USA," and my identity was securely rooted there...until it wasn't.

Everything that seemingly shaped my life had its beginnings on Killarney Road. The metal black-and-white street sign that stood proudly over the concrete corner in front of my little house identified my place in the world: the corner of Killarney and Monroe. These names had a significant history, but I never knew the provenance of how the streets were named. Killarney is a town in County Kerry, southwestern Ireland. Monroe was first used as a name by ancestors of the Pictish tribe of ancient Scotland. Although Scotland and Ireland are on the other side of the world, their influence in my life had been a recurring theme, and one that felt anything but random. As I grew up, I always knew subconsciously that these places held some deep kind of significance for me. Living at the "crossroads of Scotland and Ireland'" made it even more evident that Killarney Road was where I was "supposed to be."

> *Friendship is unnecessary, like philosophy, like art. It has no survival value; rather, it is one of those things which gives value to survival.*

> —C.S. Lewis

I was fortunate to find some of my very best friends, Beth Ann and Lisa, at the end of my cul-de-sac, on Killarney Road. When my family moved into the neighborhood when I was three, Beth

Chapter 2: Second Chance

Ann already lived in the little brown house at the end of the street. She came from a large Catholic family, the youngest of two older brothers and two older sisters. There was a baby, Andrea, who had been born a few years before Beth Ann, but she had died in infancy. On a high shelf in Beth Ann's bedroom stood a beautiful, lifelike porcelain doll, dressed in ornate white satin, with a hauntingly realistic face and long dark hair. She looked like an angel; they named her "Andrea." Whenever Andrea came down from the shelf, everyone's tone changed to a quiet, reverent whisper, as if they were in church. I was too young at that time to understand the gravity of that type of loss, but I did know there was something very special and sacred about that doll.

Both Beth Ann and I were tall, skinny blondes with freckles on our noses. Standing next to each other, we could have been sisters. Throughout our elementary and middle-school years, we were inseparable. Early on, my orphan heart found a safe haven in the childhood friends of Killarney Road. This endearing homestead not only held my fondest childhood memories, but the skeletons in my closet.

Sticks and Stones

Words are unbelievably powerful. Whoever coined the phrase (which was taken from a nineteenth-century children's rhyme) "sticks and stones may break your bones, but words can never harm you," was sadly mistaken. There is a wealth of evidence that words can, indeed, wound. Noxious words can break your spirit, like a hostile invader of mind demanding you alter the way you see yourself. Orphan-hearted people often are held captive in the dark rooms of self-doubt and reinforced negative self-talk. Piercing, unrestrained, combustible words can morph into a relentless taskmaster that replays negative voices like an evil circus trainer with whip in hand. One of the downsides of having an acute

The Secret Identity of Chance

memory is that there are things I wish I could forget. Regrettably, the way in which I learned I was adopted is one of them.

On a typical California summer day, my seven-year-old self woke up early, jumped out of bed, ran to the kitchen to gulp down my Tang and Apple Jacks, and headed to Beth Ann's house to see what big adventures the neighborhood kids of Killarney Road had cooked up for the day. Most of our mornings started out with riding our bikes through the orange groves. The joyful innocence of childhood was being with my friends, riding my banana-seat bicycle pedaling as fast as I could, watching the shocking-pink handlebar streamers flap ferociously in the wind alongside me. However, the Valencia orange grove landowners were less than thrilled about a bunch of ragtag kids skidding through their carefully manicured citrus groves on their super-cool bikes. This particular day, we were riding through the groves—or, a better description would be, we were "being chased out of the groves"—as we abruptly changed course and frantically raced home. Nothing was better after a long bike ride in the scorching sun than cooling off with an ice-cold Popsicle. Over the summer, my mom always kept a handy stockpile in the freezer. Little did I know on that delightful summer day, riding home amid sweet, effervescent orange blossoms, the warm summer breeze blowing in my face, that a ghastly secret was lurking around the corner, and my secure, perfect little world was about to crumble.

Once we returned to my house, I tossed my bike down, pulled off my dirty shoes and socks, and ran into the house to grab a handful of icy treats. Cherry was my favorite flavor, and I carefully tucked one aside before passing around the rest. We were all laughing and playing, slurping down our Popsicles, when out of the blue, one of the girls blurted out, "Did you know your real parents didn't want you, and you were adopted? Your mom and dad are not your real parents. Your real parents didn't want you, so they gave you away."

Chapter 2: Second Chance

It was like a slow-motion "drive-by." Words are powerful, and those words struck me like a bullet out of nowhere, aimed straight at me—without any rhyme or reason. *Bang, bang!* I stood there, frozen, bewildered, and confused. Stunned, I dropped my cherry Popsicle on the hot concrete beneath my bare feet. Looking down, I watched it slowly melt as the kids surrounding me awkwardly stared, as if waiting for a justifiable response. I didn't have one. My face flushed; tears of shame and embarrassment trickled down my freckled cheeks as salty droplets rolled onto the ground alongside my melting Popsicle. I did the only thing I could . . . I ran into my house, looking for "my mom."

A Little Help from a Hershey Bar

Throwing open the front door and wiping my eyes, I called everywhere, looking for my mom to tell her the awful "untruth" one of the mean kids had said, knowing she would comfort me and put my topsy-turvy world back in order.

What happened next was both unexpected and inexplicable. The first thing my mom did was to make a phone call to (I'm assuming) the mother of the child who had turned my world upside down. We had a pink, wall-mounted rotary phone that hung on the wall right above the kitchen sink. It had a cord that seemed to extend for miles, because my mom would stretch that phone cord from the kitchen clear to another room in the house whenever she needed privacy. My mom was a formidable, Irish-blooded woman; let's just say, "diplomacy" was not her strong suit when her feathers got ruffled . . . and boy, were they ruffled that day! I don't know what that conversation sounded like—and I probably wouldn't want to know.

I sat alone in the living room waiting for her to return, staring at the ironing board and the stack of wrinkled clothes she had quickly set aside to deal with my sudden emergency. As was the

The Secret Identity of Chance

custom in our family, my mom would hide our favorite treats around the house to be saved for special occasions. After hanging up the phone, she slowly walked to the freezer; my heart dropped a little, knowing what was hidden there.

That's where she kept the coveted Jumbo-Sized Chocolate Hershey Bar with almonds (which was "secretly" hidden out of sight behind the frozen peas and carrots). Hearing my mom rooting around the freezer, I knew something "very serious" was about to go down.

There are certain excruciating truths in life, and as much as we wish we could shelter our kids from them all, we cannot. This was the beginning of the painful roller-coaster ride of shocking truths that would become my life. My mom returned to the living room and sat down beside me on the black faux-leather couch. Her bloodshot eyes and furrowed brow revealed an emotional agony I will never forget.

As I nervously fidgeted, my small feet dangled off the edge of the couch, grazing my bare toes atop the thick, golden shag carpet beneath them. As she wrapped her arms tightly around me, her voice began to crack while she slowly peeled back the brown paper wrapper from the giant chocolate bar and broke off several small squares for me to pop in my mouth. As the sweet chocolate melted on my tongue, I sat paralyzed, watching my mom try her best to backpedal from what was supposed to be a very special mother-daughter moment (which she had planned since the day I was born), to frantically trying to save my tender heart from a devastating break. Resting in her other hand was a neatly folded, black-and-white newspaper article pulled out of a small white envelope, with "Marla Sue" written on the front. As she carefully extracted the mysterious article from the envelope, the floral scent of rose permeated the air. My mom frequently tucked rose oil sachets in the drawers that held her sentimental keepsakes, and it was clear this yellowed newspaper clipping

Chapter 2: Second Chance

had been intentionally pressed and saved in anticipation of this deeply meaningful conversation she knew we would eventually have when I was old enough. The heading on the newspaper article was "Dear Abby." Before dying at the ripe old age of ninety-four, "Dear Abby" was America's favorite advice columnist. Her real name was Pauline Phillips, and her Dear Abby column was read by tens of millions. My mom never missed reading her work. Sometime after I was born, a mother wrote in asking for advice on how to explain to her young daughter that she was not their biological child, but adopted. Dear Abby wrote a lengthy, heartfelt response, and my mom, with unfaltering resolve, read me the entire article, verbatim.

Mom did her best to reassure me that although other babies were born into a family, I was *special* because they chose me. But it never felt special. The careless words that had already been spoken over me as a child, telling me I was "unwanted," became my kryptonite. In many ways, it crippled me from seeing myself any differently, and like a shadow, it followed me throughout my adolescence and into adulthood, leaving me with a thousand questions no one could answer. I'm not sure what the tipping point was, but somewhere I embraced the belief that if I was truly special, my biological parents wouldn't have given me away—because you only get rid of things that have no value.

There are different levels of pain found in truth, and every human being has had to face the receiving end of it. Some truths can prick like a needle—it stings going in as you feel the intense effects of it immediately, and then it's over. You slap a proverbial Band-Aid on it and move on.

Hard truths are different. Unlike the stinging prick of truth, mine was more like an ill-flavored pill that was forced down my throat against my will. The shocking reality that I was "unwanted" became a belief that lodged itself inside my sense of identity like a

The Secret Identity of Chance

pill, left to slowly dissolve. I couldn't reject it, I couldn't change it, I couldn't spit it out.

Unchallenged, this debilitating belief attained the ability to destroy me, from the inside out.

Chapter 3

Chance Remembrance

Since discovering I was adopted, birthdays became less of a day I excitedly anticipated, and more like a day I wished I could have avoided entirely. Prior to learning I was adopted, my birthdays had been filled with vividly fond memories as our family traditionally would spend them on the beaches of Southern California. Birthdays thereafter felt confusing and different. As I got older, it became a painful reminder that I came from parents I didn't know; I had questions, and no answers. Consequently, about a week prior to my birthday each year, a mystifying sorrow always began to creep up. I wondered if my birth mother or father remembered me on this day. What were they doing? Who were they? Why did they leave me at the hospital after I was born? For whatever reason, my deep feelings of loss seemed to manifest much more intensely on and around my birthday. The innocent thrill of childhood birthdays had given way to a kind of unsettled sadness, one I couldn't quite shake off, so ultimately, I just learned to hide it.

What the heart has once known, it shall never forget.

After I walked in the front door from junior high school one day, my mom sat me down to share a story that perhaps she thought I was then old enough to understand. Our little house on Killarney Road was a stone's throw away from my elementary school. The school was lined with towering pine trees, and a large grassy field sat right behind the school building encased by a chain-link

The Secret Identity of Chance

fence (which became the neighborhood's private playground when school was not in session). If you've lived next to a school, you know there are sights and sounds that become commonplace—the line of cars parked for pickup and drop-off, playground whistles, school bells, school buses bustling in and out, the ping of tetherball chains against metal poles, and the shrieks of children laughing and playing. These were all daily activities to which I became accustomed. Another common happening was cars that parked in the school parking lot over the weekends, mostly for the use of the community basketball courts, which made this bizarre happening hard to identify at first.

Soon after we moved to Orange County when I was just a toddler, an odd recurrence began to take place. In the midst of a constant stream of random cars coming and going, my mother noticed a large sedan would pull into the school parking lot facing our house—then park. Inside sat an older woman with a younger blond woman. They remained in the car all day and never got out, and at dusk they disappeared. These anonymous strangers appeared only once a year, until I was about five or six. At some point, my mother realized the day they mysteriously reappeared each year was on my birthday. My mother was quite certain these were the same women who had been walking out of the hospital crying the day my parents came to pick me up and take me home. She believed this was my biological mother and grandmother. She made the decision that when they pulled into the school parking lot the following year on my birthday, she would cross the street and introduce herself. But they never returned after that.

There must be other (secondary) losses that add a measure of grief to a natural mother who has had to make the unbearable decision to abandon her child. It was my birthday, and perhaps this was the closest she could get to me. Sitting in an empty parking lot in the heat of an August summer day, perhaps she was

Chapter 3: Chance Remembrance

just hoping to get a glimpse of the life she created but she would never get to celebrate.

Chapter 4

Leave to Chance

*My barn having burned down, I
can now see the moon.*

—Mizuta

Blazing fires can be incomprehensibly destructive, rising up in a gust of wind seemingly out of nowhere and destroying everything—and everyone—in its path. Deadly wildfires can begin with something as innocent as a downed power line, or as neglectful as a carelessly tossed cigarette butt. A small, insignificant spark, combined with tinder-dry forests and howling winds, is more than enough to ignite a catastrophic wildfire. And once a fire begins, it can spread, consuming everything in its path, taking on a life of its own.

I was in elementary school during the early 1970s, when the home craft craze of the hippie-style psychedelic sand candles hit. These colorful images of wax creations were commonly embedded with glitter, daisies, dried wildflowers, and seashells. They fascinated me. One year, I was determined to try my hand at making the most spectacular candle ever made for Mother's Day (kids, don't try this at home!). I calculated that if I took my entire box of sixty-four Crayola crayons and carefully peeled all the paper labels off and plopped them into my mother's very best pot on high heat, they would instantly melt down into the most dazzling assortment of spectacular colors. Wrong! Right before my eyes, my beautiful sixty-four-piece set of rainbow-colored crayons melted down into what was the visual equivalent

The Secret Identity of Chance

of a muddy swamp bottom. My only saving grace was that it was going to be a "scented candle," and maybe Mom wouldn't notice the awful color if it smelled really good. Someone had given me a bottle of Love's Fresh Lemon Cologne, which I was saving for a very special occasion. This seemed worthy of sacrificing my very first and only bottle of "perfume." I carefully unscrewed the silver dome-shaped top and doused the entire glass bottle over the gas fire and into the boiling pot of wax. In one second, the combustion from the alcohol in the cologne hit the fire and sent everything ablaze! Terrified, I remained totally paralyzed, and unable to scream or even run for help.

Just then, my dad walked in from the garage and took control of the situation, extinguishing the fire. To this day, if you're lighting a BBQ, or starting a gas fire, you'll find me cheering you on from a safe distance. The fear of that experience has never left me, and I've learned a healthy respect for combustible dangers. Fortunately, no real damage was done, aside from my pride, of course, and a pretty stern (and well-deserved) talking-to from my parents.

Unfortunately, that wasn't the only combustible fire that hit my family growing up. Just as a tinder-dry forest can turn a spark into catastrophic ruins, so vulnerable is a loving family when the marital relationship between husband and wife has been left dry, unattended, neglected, and improperly cared for. It becomes "emotional kindling," and a tiny spark may be all it takes to bring ruin. I was too young to remember any conflict between my parents; I think I was only about five years old when my daddy left. I couldn't tell you what happened, or when it happened, because one day he was just gone. He moved out, and that was the beginning of many relational firestorms to come. I never saw it coming, but it destroyed everything in its path. To call it a contentious divorce would be an understatement. My dad had been madly in love with my mother, and I think those feelings remained

Chapter 4: Leave to Chance

on some level for the rest of his life. He never wanted to leave, and he never fully recovered.

After my dad "disappeared," I would often wander out to the garage looking for him. I missed hearing him whistling a happy tune while working over his hand-carved, wooden workbench. He was always tinkering in the garage or fixing something. I secretly hoped I would swing open the garage door one day, and he would be standing there, but he never was. Missing him walk through the front door after work each day calling my name, and running into his arms was agonizing. The crushing emotional confusion of abandonment can sear your soul like a third-degree burn, and it's the kind that leaves a scar. Although nobody starts a family with the intention of destroying it, just like the damage from wildfires, the most vulnerable creatures are the ones too small to care for themselves; they are at the highest risk of not escaping the devastation unharmed.

This is true for every person who has grown up as a child of divorce. Nobody escapes unscathed; nor did I.

I'll remember you, though. I remember everyone that leaves.

—Lilo and Stitch

Eventually, the pain of leaving us became so unbearable that my dad moved away. He took a new job in Northern California, where he remained until I was well out of high school. It wasn't like he moved across the world, but it might as well have been. I started to see him less and less, and then hardly at all. Being so young, I hadn't yet learned that I was adopted, or the abandonment issues I would later have to face, but I fully understood my daddy leaving and never coming home.

Killarney Road had always been my safe place in the world, but now it felt like it would never be safe again. What exacerbat-

The Secret Identity of Chance

ed the suffering was feeling torn between two parents and the emotional tug-of-war.

As a child, I didn't have the developmental fortitude to run into such a battle and win, because winning meant living with the guilt of destroying one of the two people I loved most in the world. A vast majority of orphan-hearted adults are those who were emotionally abandoned as children, and many were left on the battlefields of divorce.

Visitations were limited to sporadic weekends when Dad's work allowed him to drive down to Orange County. I developed a ritual every time he visited. He normally came on a Saturday, unless it was during the summer. I would get up early and race out the door to find the perfect spot under the big eucalyptus tree in our front yard, and I would sit . . . all day, and wait.

Eventually, my friends would come out to play and hang out with me. They would ride their bikes and skateboards and talk to me, but they knew my daddy was coming, so I wouldn't leave my spot. This may not seem like a terribly odd thing, except that he was coming from San Jose and normally didn't arrive until late afternoon, or sometimes early evening. Once I saw his avocado-green Chevrolet El Camino coming around the corner, my squeals of sheer joy could be heard for miles! Jumping up, I would run as fast as I could alongside that big green car until it came to a full stop right in front of our house. There was such a temporary sense of security and feeling of normalcy just being together again.

However, as much joy as it brought me to feel loved and safe again with my dad, in the background, the fear of the "looming good-bye" was always lurking about in the pit of my stomach, like the terrible ending to a movie that you know is coming. Saying good-bye and not knowing when I would see my dad again was an excruciating ordeal for me for as long as I can remember. Just as I would sit in anticipation and wait for him to arrive, I would

Chapter 4: Leave to Chance

sit in the same spot, inconsolable, watching his car drive away, not willing to leave until my mom came out and brought me into the house.

Somewhere in my little girl's mind, I thought he would turn around and come back for me, but he never did. The landscape was very different than it is today, and at that time I didn't know a single other kid with divorced parents. I had to wrestle with it on my own, and perhaps this is where I started my journey with God, and *the still, small voice.*

I got a bit older, and both my parents remarried (several times), and things changed. However, one thing did not change: it never got easier for me to let go of people I love and saying "good-bye" always felt crippling. There are a lot of things in life that are not worth battling over; people, however, and our relationships are worth the fight. I've learned through the course of my life that I am a peacemaker at my very core, but there are times when you have to lay down your peace sign and pick up your sword. The basis for going into any battle should never be more about who you will destroy, as much as it should be about who you will save.

Chapter 5

Take a Chance

As I grew older, marriage never felt like a viable option for me. My home life was confusing, fragmented, and chaotic, riddled with anxiety for fear of being catapulted into another step- relationship anytime I saw conflict. I learned to adapt and pivot . . . quickly. Most importantly, however, I learned to become for my three younger brothers the stable parental figure I wished someone had been for me growing up. This was an intentional decision I made very early on, and it is largely the reason I am who I am today. Unfortunately, it also created a misbelief that I didn't possess what was necessary to ever commit to marriage. I was a runner. I saw too much; I'd lived through too much. Nevertheless, I found myself stuck between two truths: I made up a story in my mind to try to protect myself, and I framed this belief around the fact that eventually everyone leaves. Then I made up rules around that belief, one of them being that I would never be able to fully give my heart to someone, or seriously commit, because it would only lead to heartbreak and abandonment. Yet, there was an even stronger truth that I held on to, one that I wanted to believe: that "somewhere out there," a love existed that could stand the test of time. My heart had its fragility anchored in resilience, and out of these two separate truths, I threw my hat in the ring called hope. In 1994, while working for the same company, I fell in love with a man I ended up marrying.

We married in November of the following year in a traditional ceremonial setting nestled in a charming and stately, old gray-stone Scottish chapel. I was strangely drawn to this little

Scottish chapel the moment I drove up. I couldn't tell you why I felt such an emotional connection; I just did. It was nothing like the church I had envisioned getting married in. I had always thought if I ever married, it would be by the ocean, but like so many other mysterious things in my life, this somehow just "felt right." As I arrived on the church grounds that crisp fall morning to help set up for the wedding reception, there was a Scottish coronation taking place. Beautiful young girls dressed in long emerald-green velvet gowns were standing in procession waiting to walk through the massive wooden doors as the thunderous tenor of bagpipes played in the background. I felt such an emotional connection to the melodic sounds of these intriguing Celtic instruments, as if they were almost destined to be there on this very momentous day.

A baby fills a place in your heart that you never knew was empty.

The stark realities of marital life kicked in pretty quickly, as I was a new bride with a husband who traveled abroad for sometimes a month on end. The "honeymoon phase" was far different from what I had imagined. Although I managed on my own just fine, there was still a hollow space that left me yearning.

When year four of married life rolled around, something quite unexpected gripped me: maternal instincts! I carried my naivete right across the marriage threshold and into marital life, thinking that being a wife would fill up all the empty places. Any type of childhood abandonment will carry a sorrowfulness that rears its ugly head from time to time. Mine would appear reminding me that I was biologically different from everyone else in my family. My two younger brothers and their biological parents (my stepparents) shared a cohesiveness that was wrapped up in their shared DNA. This created vulnerabilities, rooted in the knowledge

Chapter 5: Take a Chance

that as much as I dearly loved my family, and they loved me, they were interconnected by their ancestry; and no matter how hard I tried, I would always be excluded by the unalterable reality of genetics. I longed to have someone of my very own. Several years into my marriage, I developed an aching emptiness in my heart. I'd never felt such a deep, desperate yearning before. The anguished longing seemed to be surging from unknown places deep within me. It was relentless. I was confused. I thought being married was all I needed.

Sometimes you have to believe in what you can't yet see.

I began having vivid dreams about having a child . . . someone who was intrinsically my own. And up until this one day, that was all they were, just silly visions in my head. That all changed one early summer night when my husband and I went to dinner with friends, and what had been swirling around in my head came to life . . . so to speak. After dinner, we ended up strolling along the boardwalk to people-watch and eat ice cream. Our attention was piqued by a bright-colored pink-and-blue photo booth. Curious, we headed over to see what all the commotion was about. This wasn't just any photo booth; it was one that would accurately produce a photo of what your baby would look like based upon a couple's headshots, using algorithms and facial recognition. We were intrigued, and it seemed harmless enough, so we took the bait. We climbed in, sat down, closed the curtain, and with one bright flash, it was over. The anticipation of what "our baby" would look like was thrilling. What I didn't expect was my gut-wrenching, emotional reaction that followed. After a minute and a half, out popped a photo of the most beautiful little girl with golden-brown hair and eyes, porcelain skin, and rosy cheeks. Angelic. Oddly, she did look a bit like both of us. This visual reality moved

31

The Secret Identity of Chance

me to tears, and I secretly slipped "her" photo into my wallet for safekeeping. I could visualize a little girl just like this in my future. I could feel it in my bones! There were many meaningful conversations around the development of my deep desire to have a baby, but it wasn't my decision alone. I had married a man who was on the fence about starting a family. As time went by, I made every effort to try to find peace knowing I might never have a baby, that perhaps this aching in my heart was something with which I would simply have to live.

That all changed on August 7, 1999. We had traveled back East to visit with my in-laws over my birthday. After dinner, and dessert of homemade apple pie (made in Pa-pop's traditional communal tray), we took an evening walk around their small farm, and out of his jacket my husband handed me a small gift box to open. It was beautifully wrapped and tied with ribbon. I opened the box and peeled back the tissue paper, totally befuddled; lying inside was a tiny pair of pink and blue baby booties. I opened the accompanying letter from my husband, in which he revealed he was now ready to start a family! Goose-bumpy, I fell to my knees in the dirt and sobbed. To my astonishment, I was going to have a baby after all! The trajectory of my entire life was about to change.

What feels like the end is often the beginning.

—Anonymous

The year 1999 was a crazy time as we geared up for Y2K and all the "doomsday predictions." There was a lot of anxiety in the air as the dawn of the Millennium approached. Every news outlet suggested that due to computer glitches, the conversion to the new time period would threaten to shut down all major financial and government organizations—everyone was panicked. To make matters worse, they predicted that all transport systems would be affected, especially the airlines, whose operational flight cal-

Chapter 5: Take a Chance

culations depended upon accurate times and dates. There were even rumors that planes would drop from the sky when the clock struck midnight on December 31, 1999. This led most people to avoid travel over the holidays, especially on New Year's Eve; it was the worst time to be traveling. Regardless, the decision was made that we would continue with our travel plans to Paris the day after Christmas and stay for the New Year's 2000 celebration. Now, I was no expert, but I didn't think you could simply conceive a baby based upon your travel plans. However, my husband had had a dream months before that we would have a little girl, and that she would be conceived on this trip.

She would have brown hair and big brown eyes, and we would name her "Paris." I could have easily allowed all the Y2K fears to sidetrack me, but we celebrated New Year's Eve in the streets of Paris, and we arrived home safely.

It's always a little exhausting coming home from vacation; all the realities and responsibilities of real life are waiting at your front door. Before I knew it, a month had passed, and it was Super Bowl Sunday. Although I wouldn't consider myself a sports fanatic, Super Bowl Sunday 2000 will always have a special place in my heart. That afternoon, my sister-in-law decided she would take it upon herself to bring a box of pregnancy tests by the house. Most people bring chips and salsa, but that girl has *chutzpah!* While my husband was downstairs rooting for his favorite team, I snuck upstairs and took one, then another, and another. I stood there frozen, staring in the mirror at the absolute shock on my own face. There they were, two gorgeous, straight pink lines, as clear as a bell. Every. Single. Time. I didn't know whether to scream or cry, so I did both! I suppose I should have had some grand plan in place to "break the news" to the soon-to-be daddy, but running down the stairs screaming at the top of my lungs, "I'm pregnant! I'm pregnant!" was my knee-jerk reaction, so I went with that. We were going to have a baby!

XXVIII.IX.MM

September 28, 2000

On this day, September 28, 2000, there were an estimated 357,817 babies born (according to the data published by the United Nations Population Division). Within that astronomical number, "one" seems very insignificant... unless it's yours—and then it becomes everything. I need to assert that during my first prenatal appointment, it was confirmed that *I did, in fact, become pregnant during our trip to Paris* in December of the previous year. A hands-down miracle! *What's the "chance" of that?* I might have come into this world "accidentally," but *this* child would never brush up against such doubts. The life into which it was being born was a well-orchestrated, detailed, "prophetic" plan. This was no accident.

Soon after the first prenatal appointment, I met with the doctor to review a family health history questionnaire. I was anxious—I knew I would have to stare them down and give the same rote answer I've provided every questioning health-care professional my entire life.

"What is your family health history?" the doctor asked.

"I don't know, I was adopted at birth," I replied. Until now, this had been just my isolated reality, and the uncertainty had affected no one but me. Now the issue was far weightier—and terrifying. This time it wasn't just me who was affected; it was my unborn child. Now the unknown had anxiety and unsettling fear attached to it.

After some frightening but manageable complications in the birthing process—and a very long delivery—my baby finally arrived.

Out of my swollen womb came forth the most beautifully angelic little face I'd ever seen. At exactly 6:37 p.m., on Thursday, September 28, 2000, eight and a half pounds of miracle came out screaming. *Just like in the dream during my pregnancy*, a magnif-

Chapter 5: Take a Chance

icent healthy "baby girl with dark curly hair, porcelain skin, and big, beautiful brown eyes" was born. (Inasmuch as you have to name your baby before leaving the hospital, I was thrilled we had already made that decision in advance. *What is the "chance" of that?*)

Finally, the moment arrived, and the nurse wrapped up my brand-new baby girl and carefully laid her in my open arms, like an extravagant gift I could never afford. Holding this tiny bundle of life felt like warm, liquid love pouring over me from the top of my head to the tips of my toes. I just stared at this gorgeous creature in wonder and amazement. For someone who had never seen themselves mirrored in the eyes of another, it was astonishing. The first moment I kissed her soft, swollen little lips, I felt a literal shock of electricity bolt through my body. This baby was part of me!

As I was packing up my things to leave the hospital, I found the picture of the "Photoshop daughter" I'd kept hidden in my wallet. I picked it up and softly cradled it in the palm of my hand like I had done hundreds of times before. I stared at the worn paper photo of the mysterious smiling face I had grown strangely attached to after so long. I was grateful for the hope it had given me when I desperately needed to believe that having a baby girl of my own was a real possibility. Now I could finally let it go. I didn't need her anymore. Affectionately, I gave the picture one more glance, whispered, "Thank you," and then gently laid it by my bedside night table as I left. What I *did* take home with me, however, were the identical hospital bands my newborn and I had been fitted with immediately after delivery. She and I, as mother and daughter, were tagged with the same identifying numbers.

Those bracelets might seem like an insignificant detail to some, but to me, it was everything. Those identical hospital bracelets proved without any doubts who this child was to me—and who I was to her. We shared the same DNA, and our identifi-

The Secret Identity of Chance

cation would be forever found in each other. Unlike me, she would never have to question her origin, or to whom she belonged.

Chapter 6

One Chance in a Million

*The two most important days in your life are the day
you are born . . . and the day you find out why.*

—Mark Twain

Becoming a mother came somewhat naturally to me. This was unforeseen at the time of my adolescence. Growing up, I tried to be for my siblings what I wished someone had been for me. Assuming a parental role in the lives of my younger brothers, however, proved to be an ideal training ground for future challenges. My childhood had often been riddled with adult responsibilities at the sacrifice of a more normal, "carefree" adolescence—and this forced me to grow up quickly. The upside was that it allowed me to walk into motherhood like a skilled athlete with a lifetime of hands-on training. If getting married had been the starting line, motherhood was going to be my race.

That's not to say I had everything figured out, nor that I did it perfectly, but I was all in.

*What lies behind us and what lies before us are tiny
matters compared to what lies within us.*

—Ralph Waldo Emerson

She and I gallivanted our way through the first year, and we didn't skip a beat. I documented everything from her first grin to her first giggle, capturing it all. I never wanted to forget the small

The Secret Identity of Chance

everyday miracles wrapped up in the ordinary, because having a child of my own felt anything *but* ordinary. I pressed her first lock of curly hair between the pages of her first baby book, along with our identical hospital bracelets, and every other conceivable piece of sentimental memorabilia I could sandwich between the pages. I've kept these keepsake diaries going for many years, and someday when my daughter is older, I will plan a very special day for us to sit down and read through them together . . . maybe over a giant Hershey bar!

A happy marriage and a healthy baby felt like more than I could have ever hoped for. I had it all—so why was I constantly looking over my shoulder waiting for the other shoe to drop? And then, in one unforeseen moment, it did. Uninvited, my dreaded "why" showed up. This brazen, contemptuous voice was one I had run from all my life, and it crashed right into the middle of my "happily ever after." Although this charming description of a hyperbolic phrase that ends most fairy tales depicts the hope that grief and misfortune will stay firmly in the past, this malicious villain, "why," was coming to steal mine. Since the birth of my daughter, I had been so wrapped up in crazy joy over this new little life, there hadn't been an ounce of room to house anything but gobs of happiness—and then it happened.

When I heard my daughter shrieking in excruciating pain, I jumped out of bed in sheer panic. Her forehead was burning hot to the touch. As a new mom, my immediate response was, "Call nine-one-one!" Thankfully, reason took hold, and instead I bundled her up and rushed her to the pediatrician's office. She was diagnosed with a double ear infection and prescribed medication. Thankfully, within a short amount of time, we were safely on our way back home. Feelings of staggering relief left me wobbly from the place I'd allowed my mind to wander on that short drive to the doctor's office. Out of all the "what if" scenarios, I was beholden to the fact that an ear infection was all we were dealing with. Once

Chapter 6: One Chance in a Million

home, I bundled her up and began rocking her to sleep in the dimly lit corner of her beautifully decorated nursery as raindrops beat against the windowpanes. I cradled her tightly, feeling her tiny, pulsating heart against my chest, and her soft little head nestled in the crevasse of my neck. I promised her I would never leave her, that she was safe, that I would never let anything awful happen to her—ever. Almost immediately, a trigger switched, and the brutal question that had always haunted me was staring back at me through the innocent eyes of my own biological child. Being given up at birth now hit me on a much deeper level. Rocking her back and forth, tears tumbled down my face onto her soft pink monogrammed baby blanket. I had to face my "why." How could my biological mother have left me as a newborn? And *why?* Now that I had experienced giving birth to a baby of my own, the harsh reality seemed almost too much to bear. I'd experienced the cataclysmic shift that happens in your heart when you create a life, and I realized the vulnerability of a child who comes into the world totally helpless, dependent, and surrendered to your trust for its very survival. My exposed soul wasn't angry or bitter, just confused. I couldn't grasp the inner strength necessary to give up your child, nor did I understand the tumultuous circumstances that must have left her with no other choice. Now that I had a baby of my own, it seemed unimaginable. Abandonment was counterintuitive to every maternal instinct I had.

The statement, "Your parents gave you away because they didn't want you," came as a cruel awakening. With such a rejection, there is a certain amount of shame attached. Children typically blame themselves when something bad happens, so naturally I questioned what was "wrong with me," why my mother didn't fight for me.

Despite the fact that I grew up with all manner of relational complications due to "blended family issues," I was incredibly grateful for the family I had. However, there was never a place for me to grieve the biological family I had lost. I thought it would be too painful for my parents to see my grief, and the risk of hurting them wasn't one I was willing to take. Even as a child, I had hard questions rolling around in my head that I didn't think anyone would ever understand, so I kept them just between me and God.

Now, having a biological child of my own, I needed to "reframe" this idea of being *unwanted*. It was not just my story anymore ... but rather "our story," and I was determined to write a better story for my daughter than the one I told myself.

It's not what people call you; It's what you answer to.

—W. C. Fields

A new student showed up on the campus of our elementary school when I was in the third grade. She was petite, covered in freckles, and wore delicate floral dresses and patent leather shoes. The teacher had her sit next to me. She was sweet, but timid and painfully shy (they always put the quiet kids next to the "talkers"). Desperately wanting to make friends, she'd daily offer up her lunch money in hopes of persuading someone to sit with her (but the other kids would notoriously take her money and run off, leaving her without lunch and sitting alone). Soon I found myself elbow to elbow with her at the lunch table, sharing my peanut-butter-and-jelly sandwich, and from that day on, we became instant friends. Months later, she invited me to play at her house after school for the first time. She lived a few blocks away, and she was very excited for me to meet her dog and play on the large swing set in her backyard. We skipped together through the front door of the white tiled entryway hand-in-hand, and oddly, her mother was nowhere to be found. We walked down a long, dark hallway to her bedroom, where she pulled out a small wooden box of Barbie dolls from underneath her bed, and we carried them off to the living room to play. Caught up in laughter and giggles,

Chapter 6: One Chance in a Million

we dressed our dolls in high Barbie fashion. Then, all of a sudden, the living room door burst open violently. I looked up to see her enraged mother towering over me, red-faced and screaming a shocking rebuke at me. I sat there paralyzed. I didn't dare move, unsure what was happening. "Nobody is allowed to call her by her real name! You are only allowed to call her 'Potty'!" she yelled at me. "Until she can learn to stop wetting her pants like a pathetic little baby, she will never be called anything but Potty, do you understand me!?"

My face flushed, and my heart raced from the sheer velocity of her voice; I was stunned by her cruelty. I lowered my head, choked up by emotion, not daring to utter a word. Once her mother left the room, I hugged my friend tightly around the neck and whispered in her ear, "I will never, ever call you that. That is *not* your name!" My knobby knees knocked together for the entire three blocks home, and thereafter she only came to my house to play. Not long after, she and her family moved away. I don't know what became of her, but the cruelty of that experience has never left me. I wondered what kind of shame-based imprint that experience left on her—much like my own. I hope she grew up and became the heroine of her own story, not allowing the cruelty she suffered as a child to darken the beautiful light that was in her. It's not what people call you; it's what you answer to.

To get the full value of joy you must have someone to divide it with.

—Mark Twain

Pregnancy; Round Two

The undeniable feeling that another child was silently waiting in the wings emerged three years after my daughter was born. Baby

The Secret Identity of Chance

number two was in the works, and this pregnancy was just as well-planned and thought-out as the first. Siblings are born with an emotional frequency so finely tuned that nobody else can pick up on things the exact way a brother or sister can. They get you. They may not always like you, but they get you.

Both pregnancies posed fears that, lurking within the landscape of my family's unknown medical history, there could be serious preexisting health concerns, pregnancy complications, or genetic issues. If so, these could be potentially life-threatening for both my baby and me. "Do it scared" had become my mantra. Unbeknownst to me, though, motherhood was uniting me with a stronger, more self-confident version of myself. Where childhood insecurities and self-doubt had taken up residency, motherhood was regentrifying the neighborhood. It was becoming my new "moxie."

Although I "carried like a boy," I was secretly hoping for another girl—a baby sister for my daughter. When the much-anticipated day of arrival finally came, I just assumed baby number two would look exactly the same as our first, with dark, curly hair and big brown eyes resembling her father's side of the family. I was totally unprepared for the nurse to lay a flaxen blond–haired baby girl in my arms and say, "She looks just like her mama, but where did she get those big blue eyes?" My standard answer seemed harder to swallow this time: "I don't know." Oddly, this seemingly innocent comment instigated a 10.0 eruption in my soul that would eventually send me spiraling toward something I swore I would never, ever, do.

Chapter 6: One Chance in a Million

The Birth Certificate

It is strange, but true, that the most important turning-points of life often come at the most unexpected times and in the most unexpected ways.

—Napoleon Hill

Unimaginable joy gripped me as I walked through the front door with another beautiful baby girl. To try to express the love these precious little girls brought into my life would take a lifetime, and it would fill the library shelves of the entire civilized world. In spite of that, there was still a recurring, rather annoying, sense of distress centered around the perfectly legitimate comment the nurse had made to me at the hospital—and I wondered myself, *Where did she get those blue eyes?*

Upon returning home from the hospital, I emptied my bag and put the folder containing our birth certificates in the office for filing. The months that followed were very chaotic, adjusting to the needs of both a three-year-old and a newborn. My husband's career was taking him out of the country for weeks at a time, so I was learning to juggle motherhood on my own.

Consequently, it was a little over a year before I got back to a consistent routine and was able to catch up on projects around the house—starting with the office. Rifling through piles of paperwork, I found the small bag I'd brought home from the hospital when my second daughter was born. I remembered dropping it in the office that day; it must have gotten buried under mounds of other paperwork.

Normally, I would have filed the certificates in their designated drawer and not given it a second thought. I don't know what possessed me to open the small, letter-sized envelope that held *my* birth certificate—still in its original envelope. I'd only opened it on a few occasions when it was deemed necessary. As I slowly

The Secret Identity of Chance

pulled it out of the old, yellowed stock envelope in which it had been encased for decades, my eyes were immersed in every tiny detail while the question, *Where did she get those big blue eyes?* still rolled around in my head. I was about to seal it up and file it away for good when, upon second glance, I noticed another small slip of paper in the envelope. Believing it was just a duplicate, I'd never bothered to look at it before. But now, a strange curiosity prompted me to open it, so I carefully slid the perfectly folded document out of its envelope and slowly opened it. I recall the day my mother had relinquished it to me as a young adult, along with a particularly stern warning to never lose it.

At first glance, this document looked identical to the first. I was unfazed, and ready to fold it back up, when something unusual caught the corner of my eye. On second glance, I fixated on the emboldened black typed letters, totally confused. This was an entirely different birth certificate, with information about people I didn't know. This birth certificate represented another person named *Pauline Ann*. How did another person's birth certificate get inside *my* envelope? Oddly, the operative subject of this birth certificate had also been born on my birthday—and at the same time of day. My eyes dropped down to the box specifying the birth weight, and it was exactly the same as mine. *What was the chance of that?* Disoriented, I felt time stop as my constricting muscles tightened and my anxiety built. I nervously scrutinized this puzzling document line by line until the shocking realization crashed over me that this tiny slip of paper I *thought* had belonged to a stranger actually belonged to me. "I" was *Pauline Ann*!

Life changes in the instant. The ordinary instant.

—Joan Didion

My biological birth certificate was a sealed court record that legally should never have gotten into my hands. How did this

Chapter 6: One Chance in a Million

happen? The unfamiliar names written in black and white were my biological parents, whose identities were supposed to have been concealed from me. And why had my birth mother named me if she planned on giving me away?

I gently cradled the small slip of paper in my sweating hands, and although it had no real intrinsic value, it held the key to unlocking every question I had ever had about myself! Within a moment, that single piece of paper threw open ancient doors, and its value became incalculable. How in the world did this little stowaway document find its way into my possession? Who put it there? What should I do now? I was never supposed to see this. All my life, I'd been told my birth records were classified. Clutching the document tightly, my eyes nervously scanned it from side to side, penetrating every line, every square inch, from top to bottom. Like a soldier exploring an abandoned minefield, illusory explosions were detonating in my head, and I thought to myself, *I can't do this. I'll pretend I never found this mysterious document, file it away, and never tell a soul.* Then, suddenly, one line jumped off the page and hurled a truth arrow straight through my heart: *Name of Father.* Normally, in "secret adoptions," the biological father is rarely ever recorded on the original birth certificate. I always assumed this surely would have been the case for me, as well, but there it was . . . my father's name: "John"; his middle name, "Stuart"; and my biological family name, of *Scottish origin.* Seeing his name for the first time might have been the closest I'd ever come to love at first sight. The shock lingered for weeks.

Deep down, I sensed this discovery wasn't coincidental in any way. That birth certificate had been in my possession all my life, and I had never known it. Seeing my biological father's name in print was earth-shattering. The weeks that followed were bittersweet, as I struggled to figure out what to do next—if anything at all.

The Secret Identity of Chance

Delving into the origins of the last names of my biological mother and father, I found that my mother was Irish, and my father was Scottish—which solved the mystery of where this Celtic girl had gotten her emerald-green eyes. Interestingly, when I was growing up, my very best childhood friend was of Scottish ancestry; in adulthood, one of my very best friends—who was more like a sister—Ginger, was a "very" Irish girl. I called her my "Gingie." She was strong, fearless, and very proud of her Irish heritage. I'd never known her to cower before anything, even an unforeseen cancer diagnosis. For decades, she'd been my right hand, and I was her left. I wonder now if she cosmically subconsciously knew I had some Irish in me, and that's why we instantly clicked—and whether that's why I always seemed to gravitate to specific types of people.

Your story has the power to change the direction of someone else's story.

Invariably, the first thing people ask me when I tell them I was adopted is, "Have you ever tried to find your biological parents?" Awkwardly, I dodge this question whenever possible. Although I love my adopted family deeply, we, like many other families, fell prey to woefully complicated relational fractures. We toiled together through decades of heartbreak and betrayals from which most families would never bounce back.

In every family, there are specific roles we play, and I realized in my elementary-school years that I was the "peacekeeper" and the "mediator." Untangling conflicts, finding resolve, making sense out of madness, and ultimately "keeping the herd together" was my gift—but it didn't come without a cost. Few have been as bruised and bloodied on the battlefields of family reconciliation and forgiveness as I have, and I have the scars to prove it. This

Chapter 6: One Chance in a Million

would explain why the thought of opening another preverbal "can of familial worms" seemed too risky for me.

After a month, I'd only told a few trusted friends and family members about finding my original birth records. I was scared to even speak the words it out loud. It was too raw, and I felt too vulnerable, but the inexhaustible storyboards I was haphazardly piecing together in my head about my birth parents and all the complex possibilities were consuming me, driving me to distraction. The thought of searching for my birth parents now, after all this time, was colossal, but the relentless pull in that direction was overpowering.

Sometime over the course of that year, a popular movie came out based upon a very popular Broadway musical, and although I wouldn't classify it a "horror" movie, that may have been questionable through the innocent eyes of a three-year-old. Without my knowledge or intent, my daughter was allowed to watch this movie. Needless to say, I came home that day to a terrified toddler. She would not leave my side for one minute, frightened that the dark, scary villain would appear out of nowhere and harm her. As a result, I had to literally escort her everywhere, even within the safe confines of our home. This went on from the moment she woke up until the moment she went to bed. Soon we were both exhausted. I tried everything to get her to understand that the movie wasn't real, to no avail. Desperate, I thought that if I could find some photographs of the actor who played the villain out of costume, she would understand it was just pretend, that there was nothing to fear. After putting the girls to bed one night, I went online to search for such photographs. I was so preoccupied with the current state my daughter was in, that it never dawned on me that this "treasure hunt" was actually to settle my own heart. Scrolling through a sea of paparazzi-crazed photos of him, I stumbled upon an interview written by a BBC publication. In the article, the interviewer asked about his childhood growing up in

Scotland. It all seemed very neat and tidy, until he started sharing his first encounter with his biological father. Captivated by the subject matter, I intensely pored over every word thereafter. He told about how at a very young age, it was made known to him that his father was deceased, only to learn his father was actually alive when he hit his early teens.

What dislodged my emotional defenses was the description of the "first encounter" that took place between him and his father. He explained in painstaking detail the utter shock of learning his father was alive, and he described their four- or five-hour meeting in a pub one afternoon in Scotland. He was so paralyzed with emotion that he couldn't utter a single word back to his father throughout the entire duration of their visit. The eyes of my heart could wholly envision such vulnerability. I imagined how he might have sat there unguarded, subdued by emotion, staring into the face of a stranger but seeing his own likeness, holding on to every expression and inflection of his voice as the father narrated the adventures of a life apart from a child he'd never known. I wavered to the tension and release of this story much like an expert archer would slowly draw back his bow, and with one swift release, a gut-wrenching arrow of empathetic relatability came straight for my own heart. It pierced me through, and the sting of it lasted for days.

Why did this seemingly random account resonate with me in such an extrasensory way? I inserted myself into someone else's story, and I saw my own reflection. Whether it was the type of man, the shocking reality of discovering the identity of a biological father, or the emotional encounter upon their first meeting, it brushed up against a mystifying familiarity within my own soul that made no logical sense. But try as I might, I couldn't shake it. I've heard dozens of stories of children finding their birth parents—some are heartrending and powerful, some are destructive and disastrous—but they never moved me the way this story did. It unhinged something within me.

In the end, we only regret the chances we didn't take.

I was either going to muster up the courage to find my birth parents despite my fear and trepidation, opening myself up to the terrifying "what if's," or I would slam the door shut and never look back. The problem was, I wasn't fearless like my best friend, Gingie. I was the one who couldn't sit through scary movies, and I closed my eyes on roller coasters. I drove under the speed limit, and I have been known to toss food out well before its expiration date (just in case). My childhood was a constant adjustment to the proverbial rug being pulled out from underneath me, so keeping my feet firmly planted on the ground always felt much safer. When it came to decision-making, I sheltered on the cautious side of the street. I was the quintessential fraidy cat. I had hoped my husband would infuse me with some much-needed courage, but to the contrary, his input was to abandon the entire ordeal at the risk of finding out that my biological parents were, "worst-case scenario, drug addicts or criminals."

There was clearly risk involved. This was deeply personal, and as much as I wished I had my husband's initial support, I had to follow my own heart. That day, I made two promises to myself. First, should my search unveil an unfortunate calamity, I would remain solid and grounded in who I was, and I would not allow it to "redefine" my identity in a negative way. I was already the "me" I was meant to be. Second, I would lead with love and allow grace to open the door without judgment. Whatever the circumstances surrounding my genesis were, I had been given life, and how I got here was inconsequential; what I did with my life was entirely up to me.

The Secret Identity of Chance

But what if my husband was right? Maybe they didn't want to be found? Maybe they were dangerous people? But, then again, maybe they weren't. After weighing it all out, too many *coincidences* kept pointing me in the same direction. In my soul, I kept hearing a whisper from a "still, small voice": *Keep moving forward.*

> *There are only two ways to live your life. One is as though nothing is a miracle. The other is as though everything is a miracle.*
>
> —Albert Einstein

I have always understood that the padlocking of my original birth records protected the identity of my biological parents and the integrity of the adoptive process. However, in 2004, social networking took a quantum leap forward when Facebook went public and changed forever the way we share personal information. Needless to say, the advancements of social media, the internet, and now genealogy websites, which allow searches for family history, make it much easier.

However, sealed court records of closed adoptions were said to be nearly impossible to uncover, and I prepared myself that the search-by-name directory for my parents could be daunting. I went online to research the various ways people located their birth parents; the lists were exhausting, not to mention expensive, often requiring legal assistance and private detectives. All I had were the names of two complete strangers. As painful as it was to accept the fact that the mother who gave birth to me had given me away, I also tried to reconcile where my father fit into the scenario. From the moment my father's name leaped off the document page, it steadily beckoned to me—but who, then, should I search out first, my mother or my father? Like the North Star pointing me in one clear direction, I sensed a voice within: *Go the way of your father.*

Chapter 6: One Chance in a Million

Overwhelmed at the sheer enormity of the task at hand, as well as the endless possibilities, I did what any unsuspecting and thoroughly confused person does: I Googled it! I carefully typed my father's name into the Google search bar while uttering, "I need a miracle," under my breath. The nerve-racking seconds seemed to drag on forever before the final search results popped up: over a million hits. *Wait, what!?* How could there possibly be over a million different men with the same name? Did that mean there were a million different rabbit trails to chase down, and a million different, potentially painful rejections? I wasn't expecting this task to necessarily be a walk in the park, but I sure wasn't anticipating an exhaustive climb up Mount Kilimanjaro either. Feeling defeated from the get-go and with my hopes withering quickly, I arbitrarily picked the very first "one out of a million" from the Google search results. I landed on what appeared to be a facility staff listing for an adult school in a town in Northern California. According to the staff directory, this man was a counselor for the school. I realized there were a million other possible identifiable matches—it was like searching for a needle in a haystack, but what should I do now?

It was early August, and the emotional heaviness began to fall again like a mist. I was fast approaching yet another birthday, but even among the well-intended celebrations planned by friends and family members, the fluttering wings of melancholy hovered midair and lingered for days. My troubled mind was relieved once the day of my birth was finally over, and these menacing thoughts of abandonment took flight, heading south for the winter. But as certain as the recurring seasons were, the fluttering wings of sadness would assuredly migrate back around at this very same time next year.

This mysterious document, which had been bestowed upon me like a treasure map, would either chart my course for a new horizon or land me on the jagged rocks of rejection. Either

The Secret Identity of Chance

way, I was resolute: I would hoist my sails and set out on the precarious voyage toward an uncertain destination. I wish I could have channeled my inner Sherlock Holmes and come up with a foolproof plan, but making an "anonymous" phone call to the adult school where this man currently worked seemed like a reasonable start. I batted around what that improbable conversation might sound like in my head, as my rattled nerves were momentarily settled, remembering there were still 999,999 other possibilities if this didn't work. This was only the first "drop in the bucket." The "what ifs" overwhelmed me. I felt fenced in by a familiar anxiety, one I remembered well from childhood.

During the summers when I was growing up, my parents would occasionally drop my best friend and me off at the local YMCA pool for the day. It was a local hangout for many of the neighborhood kids, and it was always great fun—with the exception of one thing, the dreaded high dive! With the strong smell of chlorinated water in my nostrils, and the cold, wet concrete under my bare feet, I would jump right in and patiently splash around the Olympic–sized swimming pool to avoid the high dive for as long as humanly possible, hoping nobody would notice. They did. Eventually I had to face the ridicule of being the only kid who was too scared to go up, and I would find myself having to succumb to the terrifying "jump of death," as kids referred to it. Petrified, I made my way up the monstrous climb to the top, knowing that when I got there, "walking the plank" was the only way down if I was going to maintain any self-respect and avoid relentless teasing. Holding my breath, I timidly inched my way down the long board, one tiny step at a time, as my nerve endings twitched, battering my mind with instinctive messages that this was a really bad idea, only to find myself standing, toes curled around the terrifying edge of the high dive, looking straight down. There I stood, frozen, panicked, with my bony knees knocking together. I nervously stammered a childlike prayer under my breath, realizing it was too late to turn

Chapter 6: One Chance in a Million

back. Then came the split second when even though my anxiety continued to build, and fear had sapped my body of its strength, I had to surrender. I had to jump.

Contemplating the courage it would take to make such an unimaginable phone call to my potential "father" felt exactly the same. It could have ended up in a painful belly flop, but I was teetering at the precipice, and I had to jump. It was now or never. I picked up the phone and dialed the number, then panicked and abruptly hung up before anyone could answer. Suddenly, a strange calm washed over me, and although my hands were still shaking, it gave me the courage to slowly pick up the phone and redial the number. As I waited for an answer, I felt like a child again, hurtling through the air from the altitude of the high dive. On the third ring, a woman answered. Her name was Lucia.

Her voice was warm and kind. A reassuring sense of relief came over me, like the triumphant plunge into the safety of the cool, refreshing waters.

After trying to gulp down the annoying frog in my throat, I introduced myself. I explained that I was looking for an employee who worked at the school, that I had a personal correspondence I hoped to mail to him. She politely told me that unfortunately, due to security protocols, they could not give out any personal information. Sadly, however, she said he'd retired three years prior and no longer worked there. They simply hadn't gotten around to updating their website and removing his name from the facility listing. There was an awkward pause as my heart sank, and an uncontrolled sigh of disappointment escaped. I thanked her for her time through my crackling voice and was preparing to hang up. All the while, my thoughts were swirling around the fact that it had taken everything I had to muster up the courage to make this one phone call—and I didn't have it in me to go through this another 999,999 times. Just as I was ready to hang up, Lucia interrupted, and in a sympathetic tone, she suggested, "Why don't you

The Secret Identity of Chance

send your letter to me, and I will make sure Mr. McKeown receives it unopened." I thanked her profusely, and we said our good-byes.

The Letter

As a child, I always loved the grade-school tradition of exchanging Valentine's Day cards and secretly passing them out in class. I would eagerly stay up late the night before and carefully craft a well-thought-out sentiment for each classmate, then tape a small box of multicolored candied hearts to the back of each valentine. I could barely sleep in anticipation of handing out my special cards the following day. It always feels like a special occasion to give and receive handwritten cards, and I loved the idea that we would have to "guess" who it was from.

Admittedly, if I had a "crush" or a best friend, I might have earmarked and set aside a particular valentine for them . . . and hoped I got one in return. Per our elementary-school tradition, the teachers had us tape a brown paper lunch bag (freshly decorated and hand-crafted for Valentine's Day, of course) to the tall, wooden seatback of our chairs, with our names proudly written in bold black letters. We were instructed to put our heads down on our desks and close our eyes, while row after row of students were individually called up to walk around the room and secretly drop a special card or treat in each perfectly adorned bag. I could hardly contain myself.

Although these were merely cherished mementos of youthful friendships, I've saved every sentimental letter ever written to me in a special box tucked in the back of my closet. Strangely, here I sit, decades later, as a full-grown adult staring at a blank piece of paper feeling like an insecure little girl again, struggling to unearth the perfect sentiment, and hoping beyond all reason that I get one in return.

Chapter 6: One Chance in a Million

Dear Mr. McKeown,

My name is Marla. I am at a complete loss as to how one would appropriately write a letter like this, so please forgive my feeble attempt. I am the biological daughter of Shirlee Ann. I was born on August 7, 1963, at Sutter Memorial Hospital in Sacramento, where I was placed for (closed) adoption through a private law firm in Sacramento shortly after I was born. Due to a puzzling circumstance, one which I still don't quite understand, I have only recently realized that I am in possession of my original sealed birth records. In this finding, my birth certificate states the named father as a "John McKeown." Although Google search gave me over one million different individuals that may fit this descriptive name, yours was the very first one I came to. I am kindly looking for the individual listed on my birth certificate, and should this not be you, please accept my sincerest apologies for the intrusion.

Sincerely, Marla

Looking over the letter one last time before I sealed it, I wondered if I was crazy. With more than a million hits populated by my initial search, how on earth could I believe this was anything more than a shot in the dark? Turning the letter loose felt like a boomerang. Once I released it, it had the potential to circle back around and serve me a painful blow. In any case, all that remained was the waiting game.

Chapter 7

Slim Chance

B'shert is a Yiddish word which expresses a belief that there are events and relationships that are meant by a higher force in the Universe to happen. It usually involves the idea that two people are soul mates and destined to find each other, as God synchronizes the stars to align and come together.

I marked the day when I'd mailed the letter on my calendar so I wouldn't forget, and each day at exactly 12:30 p.m., our mail carrier arrived in front of our house, where I would be waiting. Walking to the mailbox each day, I felt surprisingly hopeful that a letter might be waiting for me as I pulled down the metal latch on the mailbox lid—only to look inside and find, day after day, nothing out of the ordinary inside. I had gone into this with no expectations, yet every day that passed by with no response meant I might have to accept the fact that it simply wasn't "meant to be."

And sure enough, even waiting will end . . . if you can just wait long enough.

—William Faulkner

The waiting rooms of life can be terribly lonely and confusing places. Waiting for answers, waiting for a diagnosis, waiting for healing, waiting for a sense of normalcy to return. In another corner of my life, my Gingie was diagnosed with cancer after months of invasive testing and agonizing waiting. Now she'd begun the hellish process of chemotherapy. Her massive, untamed strawberry-blond curls gave way to stark baldness, and her robust Irish frame started to show signs of frailty. My beautifully buoyant, fearless friend and kindred spirit was now in a battle for her life. There are not many things I truly hate, but cancer is one of them; it has ripped a gaping hole in my life and savagely stolen more loved ones than I care to count. My thoughts scattered like pieces of driftwood floating through currents of potential scenarios—both good and bad. Everything else in that moment seemed less important in light of Gingie's diagnosis. To be completely known by another human being and totally loved (unconditionally) anchors incredible power to friendship, and that's what we had.

Although our dilemmas were totally different, we both found ourselves sitting in God's waiting room. Together we'd walked many dusty miles through myriad fearful and unpredictable battles; this would be no different.

Just an Ordinary Day . . .

One moment in an ordinary day can turn your life upside down, and it normally starts out just like any other day.

The autumn leaves were falling outside my kitchen window, as my fragile hopes toppled down alongside them. It had been weeks, and still I had heard nothing. Had my letter gotten lost? Had Lucia forwarded it on as promised? Was my letter hidden in a pile of junk mail? I allowed these potential scenarios to distract me from the one possibility that pained me most: that he was my father, and he had simply disregarded my letter. It took every ounce of courage I'd had to expose my vulnerable heart in a way that now felt raw, laid bare, and painfully unprotected.

About this time, Hurricane Katrina had made its second and third landfalls as a Category 5 hurricane, devastating much

Chapter 7: Slim Chance

of the U.S. Gulf Coast from Louisiana to the Florida Panhandle. For days I'd anxiously watched the major news outlets report the horrific and unfolding devastation. Rescue efforts were heartbreaking, triumphant, and exhaustive. Thousands of people had gone to bed on the eve of Katrina, completely unaware of what would befall them the following morning. The predicted forecast was a moderate storm, "nothing out of the ordinary." Weather systems—much like real life—can be unpredictable, uncontrollable, and shocking.

Mother Nature reminds us that everything can shift on a dime. Likewise, we make our best predictions, but life can turn a Category 2 storm into a Category 5 one, with no warning.

In every family, there's a particular month when it seems that everyone has a birthday—and for us, September is that month. While my husband was routinely out of the country for work and wouldn't be home for weeks at a time, I was frantically trying to juggle life and motherhood on little sleep and heaps of caffeine. On just a typical day of running behind schedule, with two little ones in tow, I dashed out the door to get my many "belated" birthday cards in the mailbox before the postal truck pulled up— only to realize I'd just missed him. Frustrated, I reached inside and scooped up the mail, then quickly sorted through the stack as I walked back into the house. Just then, my eyes caught a glimpse of a standard-size envelope tucked underneath the pile of mail in my hands.

Within seconds, proverbial sirens began sounding off in my head as my "Category 2" momentary aggravation regarding delinquent birthday cards shifted direction, elevating itself to a "Category 5" storm without any warning.

Looking around quickly, I rushed into the house and closed the door behind me as the pile of mail slipped through my hands. I frantically searched for the return address. It was from him! The address appeared to have been typed on some sort of vintage

The Secret Identity of Chance

typewriter. Taking hold of the envelope, I suddenly tossed it on top of the grand piano sitting in the center of the room like it was a hot potato, then quickly stepped back.

Anxiously, I circled the piano, never taking my fixated eyes off the letter as I reasoned in my mind that it was too far-fetched to think that this man—the very first, out of a literal million—could be my father. Finding a family member out of a closed adoption can take years and thousands of dollars in legal fees, and most still come up empty-handed. This was probably just a polite, yet awkward "Dear John letter," letting me know I had reached the wrong person. I picked it up and held it up to the light, trying to make out the contents—when I caught sight of a fully "typed" letter. As I turned it over, I saw that a piece of Scotch tape had strategically been placed over the envelope flap. I could hear my own heartbeat as I sliced it open with a sharp kitchen knife, then pulled the letter out. It was fully typed, single-spaced, on one page of onionskin paper that smelled of Old Spice. The fragrance lingered in the air as my eyes fell to the bottom of the page, where it was signed, "Sincerely Yours."

September 18, 2005

Dear Marla,

I picked up your letter a few days ago from my former secretary, Lucia, at the Berkeley Adult School and, of course, was stunned by the contents and haven't thought of much else since. I know it was difficult for you to write it not knowing what, if anything, you would get back. That is how I feel this morning as I write back to you, but I am very much hoping that we can get by that, and I can be of help to you as you try to figure out your history.

There is no doubt that I am the John McKeown that is on your adoption papers. I had no knowledge of you,

Chapter 7: Slim Chance

Marla, until I got your letter, although Shirlee tried to tell me that she'd had a baby a year or so after the fact when I ran into her one night at a local Sacramento nightclub that the folks our age frequented, but I didn't believe her. The deep sadness that I feel about that now is of no consequence to anyone but me as a 67-year-old looking back over his life and youth and grieving about the things he could have done much better.

The brief outline of the story is this: Shirlee and I both went to Sacramento High School together in the mid-fifties, although my memory of it is that Shirlee was a year ahead of me. She was one of the most popular girls in the school, very pretty and involved with the sorority and fraternity kids around which most of the social life of the school revolved. I was on the other end of the social spectrum, and although I'm sure we saw each other in passing I don't remember so much as a hello even passing between us in school during those years. We met and started going out together 6 or 7 years later when I was going to Sacramento State and trying to finish my B.A. in psychology and she was already divorced and had a 3-year-old little boy and was working for a photographer as his assistant. I was struggling at the time to try and finish college, take care of my invalid dad while my mother was working, and I was working in the State Forestry during the summers to make enough to keep going to school. Shirlee was interested in getting married again and settling down and giving married life another try. As much as anything, these wide differences in our future interests came between us, and we went our separate ways. I did finish college, stayed long enough to get my master's degree, and soon after that left for Berkeley, where I worked in the public school system for 35 years and retired several years ago. I don't know what became of Shirlee, Marla, or whether you have tried to contact her as well as me. I have been married for 32 years to my wife, Katherine, who also worked for the Berkeley Schools in special education, and she just retired herself this past June. We have no children and have lived here in El Cerrito for almost 25 years.

I would be very glad to get to know you, Marla, if you have any interest in that, exchange pictures and give you any other information that I might be able to come up with for you. Please feel free to write to me at my home or call me if you wish. Looking forward to hearing from you.

Sincerely Yours,

John McKeown

Chapter 8

Second Chance

*There will come a time when you believe everything is
finished; that will be the beginning.*

—Louis L'Amour

I closed my eyes, pressing his letter softly against my cheek
as the spicy, clove aroma of Old Spice pervading the letter filled
my nostrils. Out of nowhere, the mighty hope winds materialized
and came barreling through my identity at 200 miles per hour,
destroying every misconception and false narrative I'd ever told
myself. The only thing it left standing in the wake of its determined
path was truth. Shock and disbelief overtook me as I pored over
my father's letter, devouring every syllable, trying to let the profound weight of it sink in. Reading through the letter for the first
time, I had prepared to battle through disappointment and even
heartbreak; the thought of validation had never entered my mind.
Ever. The words, *I had no knowledge of you, Marla, until I got your
letter* sprang off the page—wait! What? If he had never known of
my existence, then he hadn't abandoned me, yet this was what
I had believed all my life. I hadn't been rejected by my father; I
had been *unknown*. Like a monster constantly lurking behind the
veiled recesses of my mind were these misbeliefs, taunting me,
created by years of painfully false constructs I'd told myself and
fully believed.

I was deeply moved by the vulnerable and transparent way in
which he had recaptured memories shared with my birth mother
decades ago, and the direct and honest way he'd attempted to give

The Secret Identity of Chance

context to my origin. Then it dawned on me; this man had spent his entire thirty-five-year teaching career helping other people's children—but he'd never had any of his own. *I am his only child.* I couldn't help but wonder . . . In *secret* adoptions, a birth father is commonly listed as "unknown." Did my mother purposely put my father's name on my original birth certificate in the hopes that someday I would search for him? Was it possible that my father and I were *supposed* to find each other all along, "b'shert"? Perhaps the still, small voice that prompted me to *"go the way of your father,"* was as much for his sake as it was for mine.

> *Life always offers you a second chance, it's called tomorrow.*
>
> —Dylan Thomas

The next day, feeling "emotionally hungover" after the shockwave of surprise that had shown up in my mailbox the day before, I reread the letter. I stared in silence at the phone number typed at the bottom of his letter, like one would assess a complex chessboard, trying to determine the next move. Whatever happened next was entirely up to me. Yet, this man, my biological father, had made it clear that he would like to hear from me. This revelation was both flabbergasting and terrifying. How would I even begin such a conversation? I decided to try to reach my husband—he was in France on a business trip and wouldn't be home for several weeks, so I ended up leaving an exuberant voice mail concerning the whirlwind events of the last few days. I felt a pang of disappointment that I couldn't reach him directly to tell him my thrilling news. However, the jarring screams and copious tears from Gingie after I read my father's letter to her over the phone helped to make up for it. She had been my unfailing confidant, one of the very few in my trusted circle who truly understood this very fragile and complicated part

Chapter 8: Second Chance

of my family dynamic. I needed bravery to make this impossible phone call, and nobody was more courageous than my Gingie. As best friends, we had just celebrated our August "Leo" birthdays, as we had done together for decades. If we were both lions, she was *the* "Lion of Judah," while I, on the other hand, was the "Cowardly Lion from the Land of Oz." Clearly, this vast difference between us was never more evident as I struggled with crippling fear and a total lack of boldness to pick up the phone and dial the number. What if I said something wrong? What if he wasn't anything like he sounded in his letter? What if his wife was upset by me just "showing up" after all this time (and who could blame her)? What if the phone call was so painfully awkward that we couldn't move past it? Despite my spiraling angst and sheer lack of confidence, Gingie stepped in like she'd done a thousand times before, talking me "down off the ledge" and giving me the courage I needed to pick up the phone and make that life-changing phone call—"what ifs and all."

Shivering, I glanced at the thermostat, set at 78 degrees, as I paced back and forth across my bedroom floor. I read through the letter one last time, looking for any signs of concern, but every carefully worded thought made me feel safe, both in his intentions in reaching out to me, and through his emotional accessibility in doing so. There were no "red flags"—not a single one.

My fingers finally dialed the number (as I secretly hoped to get his voice mail). On the fourth ring, a deep, authoritative voice answered and said, "This is John." His manner was abrupt, intimidating, and very direct. I got the immediate impression he was not the type of person who welcomed unsolicited phone calls. Grasping for words, I stammered and stuttered an awkwardly clumsy, "Hello, ahh . . . well . . . umm . . . this . . . ahh . . . this is Marla." There was a brief, uncomfortable silence on the other end of the line—and then he replied in a gentle and contemplative tone, without missing a beat, "Hello, Marla, I am very happy to

65

The Secret Identity of Chance

hear from you, my dear." Sensing the swift change of inflection in his voice once he realized it was me, I let out a huge sigh of relief. The tenderness of his greeting disarmed me and released a floodgate of pent-up emotions, which erupted without warning. I struggled to gain my composure, floundering in embarrassment. Gulping down tears, he tenderly interjected, "It's okay, darlin', it took a lot of courage for you to write that letter, and to ring me up today." His empathetic words wrapped themselves around me like a hedge of reassurance, but I realized the emotional weight of this initial conversation felt too heavy for me to carry. This gift was too big for me to open on my own.

The Gift

Christmas is a time when children instinctively gravitate toward the biggest gift under the tree. I'll never forget the shrieking sound of my daughter's three-year-old voice screeching from the top of the stairs as she looked down at the massive, oversized Christmas present waiting for her. The challenge became that the box was bigger than she was, and she struggled to get her little arms around it; she needed help even to open it. As I helped her untie the ribbons and peel back the gold-foil wrapping, there was revealed a fully furnished trilevel dollhouse inside. It was her favorite gift that Christmas, but left on her own, she would have never been able to open it.

I felt a similar frustration as I tried to peel open this miracle moment. "Wrapped up" in years of longing to know the truth, I had dreamed of this day all my life, but I was buckling under the gravity of it. Like my daughter, I, too, was frustrated with my own inability to "open" the conversation or even "get my arms around it." Realizing the weightiness was too much for me, John stepped in, and in the most "fatherly way," took over the heavy lifting in the conversation. Like a protective parent helping a struggling child,

Chapter 8: Second Chance

he lifted it right off my shoulders. He navigated the conversation, allowing me time to regroup as I began an enthralling two-hour journey into the life of this intriguing man who was my father.

He said, "The family home, in which I lived on the day you were born, was just blocks from the hospital—the same hospital I was born in myself. After high school, I earned a master's degree in psychology and administration. I was one of the large group of teachers hired during the first year of full school integration in Berkeley, and it was there that I met another new hire, my wife, Katherine. She worked in special education, and I was a school counselor. We married in 1973, and we have been very happily married ever since." As he spoke, I clung to every word, closing my eyes, trying to imagine his face. He loved animals, and they loved him, and he connected equally well with at-risk youth (particular things we both have in common). His driving empathy for kids was what led him to a career in school counseling.

He shamelessly bragged of his beloved companion, his Australian sheepdog, Chita, who accompanied him everywhere. He took a short walk into town almost every morning with Chita to FatApple's, a quaint little neighborhood bakery/restaurant where locals congregated for their morning coffee and visited.

Everyone knew Chita by name. At one point, John had been quite friendly with the goatherds who worked the Berkeley hills, and in years past, you would have found him on his buckskin quarter horse, Folly, helping to move the flock. Although Folly had since passed, she had a colt named Vito, which became the new object of my father's deepest affection. Sometimes he took his clever dog, Chita, to herd goats and ducks when the opportunity arose. Horses and horse husbandry were his passion, however, and he was masterfully and uniquely gifted for it. He boarded Vito at Coyote Ridge Ranch, somewhere on the other side of the Berkeley hills. And the ranch was where you would find him on any given day. The tonality of his voice turned low and reflective when he

67

The Secret Identity of Chance

spoke of the ranch. He told me, "I had a love for art in school, and it encouraged me to find enjoyment in creating things"; so he built an extensive workshop in his basement for woodworking and leatherworking, and he trained for years as a student in the art of growing and pruning bonsai plants under a dear friend and Japanese Bonsai master in town. He explained, "My appreciation for other cultures fueled my passion for travel, which led me on many adventurous journeys around the world. Katherine and I took a year off work and lived and traveled in a remodeled Volkswagen van touring Central America in the 1970s." And they often traveled to the Spanish Language Institute in Spain for a month or so, just to live among the locals and brush up on their language skills—and, of course, learn to play the flamenco guitar. As we began to share stories about our shared love of travel, I mentioned my memorable trip to Paris, on which I was engaged to be married, and he abruptly interrupted and asked me, "When were you in Paris?" When I answered, he said in a stunned voice, "Katherine and I were on vacation in Paris at *exactly the same time.*" *What? You have to be kidding?!* I thought. We were both silent for a few moments as this shocking revelation sank in. As I recalled that infamous Paris trip, it was almost inconceivable that I could have been sitting across the room from my biological father in our favorite Parisian café, or standing next to him in the elevator going up in the Eiffel Tower, or walking right past him on the city streets the night I was engaged, and I never knew it. It felt deeply significant—and hair-raising—that my father was there, even if I didn't know it, for such an important and momentous day in my life. *What is the "chance" of that?*

After we'd gotten past the initial introductions and bonded a bit over his life stories, the conversation shifted to family matters. I was curious about his birthday, and he told me, "My birthday is August fifth, and my father's—your grandfather's—birthday was on August twelfth." We both broke out in laughter when I told him

Chapter 8: Second Chance

that mine was August seventh! My father, grandfather, and I all had birthdays within the same week. *What is the "chance" of that?* Once our laughter subsided, I casually mentioned that he had two darling granddaughters who were fifteen months and three and a half years of age. The silence was deafening, and now he was the one grappling with emotions. He quietly whispered in a crackling voice, "I have two granddaughters?" A man who had dedicated his entire life to children, but had never had any of his own, was coming to the stark realization that he was not only a father, but a grandfather, and it overwhelmed him. Gaining his composure, he quickly segued to asking me how I was able to obtain my sealed birth records. This man was a deep critical thinker, and his mind was running precision diagnostics on every bit of information I provided. I had no idea—nor did my adoptive parents—exactly how my original birth certificate arrived in my possession. I assumed it was all within the securely sealed envelope I had been given when I was eighteen—the two slips of paper: my original birth certificate and a "copy." I never opened the "copy." This still remains a mystery.

Blessed Lucia

"Well, my dear, let me explain another miraculous set of circumstances surrounding your letter, and just what exactly it had to go through in order to reach me." My father went on to explain that on that very day, and at the exact time that I had picked up the phone to call the school (after my Google search), something was happening behind the scenes of which I had been completely unaware. Unbeknownst to me, in the five minutes before I called that afternoon, the woman who would have "normally" answered the phone was called away immediately due to an unexpected emergency.

The Secret Identity of Chance

They had nobody to cover her position, so they had asked Lucia if she would come up front and cover the phones for an hour or so. This was not her department, nor something she would normally do, but they didn't have a single other person who could step in at the last minute to fill in for the receptionist until she returned. Only because of this urgent disruption was Lucia put in the position to intercept my call. Although she had initially told me that she couldn't be of any assistance, she ended up consenting to help me. What I didn't know at the time was that Lucia had been my father's personal secretary, and a dear family friend, for almost twenty-five years. Had the woman who was assigned to be working the front desk that day not had an emergency that necessitated her leaving abruptly, allowing Lucia to step in, my letter would have never been sent. The staff receptionist didn't know my father; he had retired years before. Lucia later told him, "There was something so compelling in her voice that I knew the letter must be important." Because of their personal relationship and long-standing history, she had access to my father in a way nobody else did. It was as if a loving, sovereign hand methodically moved people and events around that afternoon with precision timing, making it an absolute certainty that my letter would get into the hands of Lucia. *What is the "chance" of that?*

After my letter arrived, Lucia called my father, who was vacationing in Red Fish Lake, Idaho, with his wife, Katherine. She told him a personal letter had arrived for him at the school. She thought it might be important, and he should pick it up as soon as he got back into town. That was the reason it took so many weeks for him to respond, although I had convinced myself otherwise. He eventually returned home while his wife stayed in Idaho to visit with her sister. Once he returned to town, my father retrieved my letter. He said, "I was devastated, and I sat on it for about three days and told no one. I opened the letter in front of Lucia, stunned. With my best 'poker face,' I brushed it off, and initially

Chapter 8: Second Chance

told her it was from a former student requesting a letter of recommendation, which was a common occurrence. I was overcome with shock, and needed time." I expressed my concern about how his wife, Katherine, responded once he finally told her the truth. He said, "Well, she laughed it off, commenting that it was preposterous." It was preposterous because my father had an iron-clad constitution, and he and his wife had been happily married for thirty-seven years, during which time he had never—and would never—step out of the marriage. However, my age clearly revealed that the relationship he'd had with my biological mother took place years before he'd ever met Katherine. Once he explained to her that I was positively his daughter, she, too, was left stunned. Having spent the entirety of her career in special education helping students improve their education and lives, but never having had a child of her own, the possibility of having grandchildren seemed inconceivable. This was earth-shattering for both of them.

John stopped mid-sentence. "Marla, there is something else I want to explain to you in more detail. I saw your mother, Shirlee, about a year after you would have been born. She was coming out of a popular club in town that many of us frequented, just as I was walking in. She was in a little black dress, looking like a million bucks alongside her date for the evening. As she passed by me, she said quietly, 'Make no mistake, John, we make beautiful children together,' and then she was gone. That was it. I never saw her again. I always wondered why she would say something so odd. It never made sense to me. She in no way looked like she'd just had a baby. I dismissed it and forgot about it through the years. Learning that you were a mere three pounds explains a lot. I had no knowledge of you, Marla, but knowing that you and your little girls have a happy life and a loving family brings me such relief." Emotions gave way as his strong, commanding voice began to crumble, straining to force out the words, "if anything would have happened to you..."

The Secret Identity of Chance

I sat in awkward silence while he tried to collect himself, then quickly segued into telling him I would put another letter in the mail soon with photos of myself and our girls. Regaining his composure, he said, "You come from a very well-documented historical ancestry, and there are a significant number of genealogical records and information on our descendants I will gather up for you, as well." As an adopted child in a family of mostly biological siblings, hearing this both confused and excited me. I had learned that my mother was Irish, but I was curious to know about my father's side, so I asked him, "What am I?" He replied, "We are proud Scots, my dear." Scottish? I thought back to the old Scottish Chapel in which I'd chosen to get married, and the feeling I'd had the minute I drove up to it—a kind of "kinship" and familiarity. John continued on to say, "I own a traditional kilt in our Tartan Clan, along with harboring a bit of a fetish for collecting Scottish swords and knives. I have in my possession a small collection. Several years ago, my sister and brother-in-law—your aunt and uncle—traveled to Scotland and visited a site where our family has the small remnant of a castle still there today. In addition, you also have a fascinating hereditary line to France. You are a *Mayflower* descendant, and your grandmother and aunts have been long-standing members of DAR—Daughters of the American Revolution." He explained that exhaustive family research had been done, along with all the required verifications to prove the family lineage, and his sister was already in the process of making copies for the girls and me.

The fact that I was somehow tethered to these hereditary organizations and societies through my actual bloodline left me feeling strangely "unqualified." The word *descendant* was not a word I identified with.

It had only been hours since we'd first said hello, and my life already felt different. In all the potential "scenarios" I had played over in my mind since I was a little girl about what my father

72

Chapter 8: Second Chance

might be like if I ever found him, nothing—and I mean nothing—even came close to the reality of this unique and intriguing man. I felt an instantaneous familiarity and connection to this kind stranger, which was both extraordinary and unsettling. I was especially amused by several of our shared innate tendencies and peculiarities. They were things I picked up on only because I had the same "bent." My father, like myself, was not one for "small talk" or idle chatter. To him, and to me, communication should be meaningful, and getting to the "bottom line" is always the end goal. Conversationally, he reached for this in much the same way I did. We both ask a lot of questions, listen carefully to what is "not" being said, and refer to stories to illuminate understanding. I pondered the things he revealed about himself, what kind of man he was, and the important characteristics he clearly wanted me to know about him. I learned much later on that his vulnerability with me was a special and sacred trust, not one he extended to many.

I referred back to the journal I had set in my lap prior to making this crucial phone call. I wrote down all the important things he'd said so I would never lose our first conversation to haphazard memory, and after almost two hours of enthralling dialogue between us, I am so thankful I did.

Looking back over my detailed impressions, scribbled notations, and nervous doodles, a few descriptors clearly stood out. He was a colorful raconteur and storyteller, with a keen intentionality that governed his every thought, fiercely protective of the vulnerable and those he loved . . . whether those be people or animals. He was also in control at all times. These were my initial takeaways, and time would tell if my first impressions were accurate.

The Secret Identity of Chance

Life shrinks or expands in proportion with one's courage.

—Anais Nin

After hanging up with my father, I found myself searching for something familiar, because everything felt different somehow. My questionable identity had been replaced with an unfamiliar, yet poignant new reality. The undeniable truth of who my father was began to shift my own self-perception and the lens through which I saw myself. Although this precarious search had had the potential of going in many disparaging directions, it hadn't. In exchange for the risk this pursuit demanded, a providential door was opened, and I was invited in. My personal narrative was evolving into the unknown, with conversations that included unfamiliar words like *descendants, genealogy,* and *lineage*—words that are foreign to most orphans and adoptees. My curiosity was superseded only by my joy over all the thrilling possibilities.

Chapter 9

Jump at the Chance

*Don't miss any chance that life gives you to jump
into unknown territory.*

—Juanma Rodriquez

If I were to be asked if my adopted family ever felt threatened by the fact that I'd found my biological father—which is a fair question—the answer would be no. My family is not only the nearest and dearest, but a mixed bag of stepsiblings, step-grandparents, stepaunts and -uncles, stepmoms and -dads, and anything and everything in between. We have sung and suffered through second and third marriages, divorces, widowhood, and all manner of blended family chaos and tribulations. We haven't done it perfectly, and there have been toilsome ups and downs along the way, situations that shook our foundations to the core, things that required miracles to overcome . . . but we did. Trying to keep the family intact was my undertaking—and a hill worth dying on. One of the benefits and blessings of our "menagerie" of blendedness was the life motto I adopted: *"It's just more people to love."* Perhaps because I have always chosen to see it that way, it allowed for an easier transition bringing my biological family into the mix. My absolute love and devotion to my adopted family was never in question. Never. And the fact that I was able to share this remarkable journey with my entire family made it all the sweeter.

The rich hues of fall ushered in the warm October Santa Anas, and I was looking forward to slowing down from the busy summer activities and centering my family around home for the

The Secret Identity of Chance

holidays. Fall is my favorite time of year, and as I found out in our last phone call, it was my father's favorite season, as well. Between my brothers and me, we ended up with five little girls and a boy, all born within a few years of each other. In keeping with my long-standing desire to keep the family close, we had decided to sell our previous homes and move into a new housing development where we could raise all our children together and secure their enrollment in the same schools. Well, actually, the "we" was me. It was *my* big idea. I guess being the big sister comes with some persuasive advantages.

Raising our kids together was a dream come true for our entire family, and having my biological father step into my life sealed it for me.

Our phone conversations became more frequent, and each time we spoke, everything became clearer. We created a sacred nightly routine when my husband was out of the country on business, which was often. I would call my father after I put the girls to bed, and we talked for hours. He was a self-professed "night owl" . . . and I was learning to be one. We had the entirety of our lives to catch up on; therefore, finding enthralling things to talk about was never an issue. The hysterical narrations of his many adventures kept me captivated, as well as the impassioned way he chronicled some of the heartaches of his youth. However, one story in particular left me speechless, dolefully revealing more about him than perhaps anything he'd ever told me about himself before, or after.

In the original letter he sent to me, he'd pointed out that he and my mother had run in different circles in high school. While she was president of several social clubs on campus, he was associated with the "rabblerousers." He took a deep breath and began to retell the fateful day when "one of the guys in our group made the disastrous decision to bring marijuana to school, and it was found. This was back in the fifties, when possession

76

Chapter 9: Jump at the Chance

of marijuana was an egregious offense." For whatever reason, my dad was chosen out of the group of teen boys and immediately ushered to the principal's office, where he was aggressively interrogated. He said, "They knew it wasn't my drugs—which I made emphatically clear—but they believed I did know who had brought it on campus, and they were right. They were determined to get it out of me one way or another. I was in absolute defiance, and they were unable to manipulate, frighten, bully, or coerce it out of me. As a last resort, they threatened to blame me for the entire incident and send me to a youth correctional facility if I didn't come forth and 'rat out' the responsible party." For my father, loyalty was the highest code of ethics.

Consequently, he took the fall for it, and he was sent away for months to pay restitution for something he didn't do. Worse yet, the administration knew full well that he didn't do it. By the time he'd served his time and returned to school, he had developed a deep distrust and dislike for authority figures, and his outward attitude reflected that. As a result, the principal informed him he wouldn't be allowed to graduate with his class because "he didn't show a repentant enough attitude." His indignant father went down to the school and advocated for him, and the principal reluctantly allowed him to graduate with his class. Soon after graduation, his parents took on a fair amount of debt by hiring an attorney on my father's behalf. Eventually, he was exonerated of all charges. I couldn't decide if this angered me more than it broke my heart. Where was this so-called friend who had allowed my father to pay so dearly for a mistake he didn't make? Why didn't he step up and admit his own wrongdoing? And what kind of justice system sends a minor away because "someone has to pay," knowing full well he didn't do the crime? Yet, it was a matter of principle for my father.

This, more than anything, explained his passion and fierce stance on a fair justice system, and most likely, it was why he got

The Secret Identity of Chance

into youth counseling. Perhaps his huge heart for at-risk youth was born out of his own childhood trauma. Where the system failed him, that was where he chose to put his stake in the ground. I zeroed in on his shifting tones of anger as he retold the story, and his emotional coat of armor appeared for the first time. Throughout his life, his personal coat of arms was built upon steel plates of indignation over those who abuse power—and the vulnerable who suffer at its hands. However, the enormous impact he made during his lengthy career, and the countless children and young adults he was able to protect from a similar fate, only proves that those who tried to bury him early on didn't know he was a seed.

We look for a horse with one chance in two of winning and which pays you three to one.

—Charlie Munger

Days later, I received a second letter, which was also typed single-spaced on a sheet of onionskin paper and smelled of Old Spice. My father only sent letters "typed' on his old, vintage Royal typewriter—and always on onionskin paper. I found something endearing and very unique about this. We are saturated in electronics. Computers are effortlessly extraordinary—you just hit the keys you want, and letters magically appear on a screen in front of you.

However, old typewriters are not so easy. They're not intuitive, and they can't edit, fix grammar, or standardize sentence structure. The fact that my father would labor on his old Royal to type out a proper correspondence made each letter feel incredibly unique and special . . . much like the man himself.

Chapter 9: Jump at the Chance

Dear Marla,

Didn't get this done yesterday as I planned, so I am doing it first thing this morning and hope these get to you by Saturday at least.

This is just a random assortment of things that came to my hand in Kath's absence. Talked to her on the phone yesterday, and she wants to put a better selection together for you when she gets back. A couple of Kathy and I at home (or one) and a couple in Yosemite, one from the Adult School just before I retired, a copy of the one my mom had taken about the time I was 20, a picture of Chita and me (my little Aussie girl who now is 15) in the mountains, and the last of Vito, my quarter horse gelding looking as you hope to be all the time with horses—no stress, no strain. I had his mother 24 years, and I've had him 14 years, since he was born. There's no rhyme nor reason to this selection, Marla, I just thought that of the ones close by, these gave a pretty good look-see at me and something of what kind of person I am. The pictures of me as an infant and child are kind of fragile after so many years, so I'm going to let Kath get them loose from the albums and put them together.

I got into horses about 25–30 years ago, and it became my, what should I say, passion or obsession, depending if you were talking to me about it or someone else,

I guess. I like horses—they like me. Vito probably saved my life a couple of years ago, Marla. If it hadn't been for him bucking me off (my fault), you might just have missed me. We got into a tangle with a big, old Angus bull named Buddy, Vito got scared, as he ran up behind us snortin' and shaking his head, and he started bucking. Took me so much by surprise that I just couldn't ever get in time with it and finally came out pretty hard, broke 4 ribs and punctured a lung with one of them as I hit the ground. Spent 5 days in the hospital, during which time they took a lot of chest shots (and back) to see how the ribs and lungs were doing. Three months later, my regular doc at Kaiser thought I should get a follow-up X-ray to see how the breaks were healing. The picture showed the breaks healing fine, but also there were three tiny cancer spots that had just shown up since I was in the hospital. That was the bad news, as there's always got to be some fly in the ointment, doesn't there? The good news is that because they found them right at the beginning and shrunk them into almost nonexistence, they are gone, and with a chemo maintenance, they are staying that way after 2 1/2 years. I have no symptoms from them except for feeling a little more fatigue and having much less hair on my head, have none from the chemo either. My doctor tells me that it is very rare for this to happen and that I should be very happy about it. Kind of hard to be happy about anything connected to it, but I'm sure she's right. If Vito hadn't bucked me off, requiring the follow-up X-ray, I would have probably gone a couple of years without knowing I had it, and then when you start to have symptoms, it's too late to do anything about it. I still do everything I always did, Marla, except for maybe hiking long distances. In every respect, I'm fine and not plannin' on leaving for some time,

Chapter 9: Jump at the Chance

so don't worry. I felt like I had to tell you, Marla, so you wouldn't get caught by surprise when we get together. All for now...get ahold of you after Kathy gets home. I've sat here for fifteen minutes looking at this, Marla, and not knowing how to sign it, but am just going to go ahead and say, Love Dad.

There was a smaller envelope tucked inside the letter with photos enclosed, but I was still trying to catch my breath and process what I'd just read. My father had cancer? I grabbed my stomach, as I'd been sucker-punched right in the gut.

Cancer isn't just a "fly in the ointment"; it's an "iceberg on the *Titanic*"! Once I read the word *cancer*, I couldn't focus on anything beyond that point. I set the letter down and stepped back from it in utter disbelief. I picked up my daughter's teddy bear she'd left on my bed and walked out to the balcony with it clenched tightly in my arms. "Teddy Bear" sleeps with my daughter every night and accompanies us to scary doctor appointments and any airplane or road trip we've ever taken, without exception. I sat on the balcony under the cool shade of the giant pines listening to the wind whistling through the trees, my arms tightly gripped around Teddy Bear. My heart hurt. How could this be? I was already walking my best friend, Gingie, through a similar battle, and now I find out my father has cancer, too? Cancer is an evil nemesis that has crashed into my life too many times, and without remorse, attacked those I love and carried them away. My heart was melting like wax within me. I was dumbstruck by disbelief. I had no other choice but to sit in the penetrating and crushing truth of this; there was nowhere to hide. In a weakened whisper, the words, "God, please," fell from my quivering lips while in subdued sadness I buried my head like a frightened child, shedding tears of anguish into the fluffy plush bear. I tried desperately to reconcile my "happily ever after," full of hopes and dreams, with the biological father for whom I'd waited all my life, against the harsh reality and fearful "what ifs" of an unforeseen cancer diagnosis. This must have been very difficult for my father to tell me—and the reason he disclosed it in a letter and not over the phone. I dried my tears and came back inside the house. I sat on the edge of my bed and reread the entire letter, start to finish this time. I pondered the shocking revelation that if my father's horse had not bucked him off that day, I might have missed him entirely. His doctor stated that it was "very rare" to detect lung cancer literally within a few short months of it manifesting in the body. I sat with this and let the implausible reality of it really sink in. How sorely devastating would it have been, had I finally found him after all these years, only to learn I'd narrowly missed him and he was already gone? Was his life miraculously spared by the merciful hand of God that day? There could be many unexplained reasons, but without question, one big reason was me.

As my thoughts began to clear, I tried to regroup and focus on the important details he had spelled out for me regarding his prognosis. I felt a deep sense of relief wash over me as I read that he'd been in remission for two and a half years with no symptoms, which is the best-case scenario. He had no traces of cancer and no limitations to speak of, and absolutely no sickness. He was alive, and for the most part, healthy; I realized I was staring down the barrel of a bona-fide miracle.

This phenomenon hit me square in the face, as tears of sadness morphed into knee-buckling tears of inexplicable gratitude. His horse, Vito, had literally saved his life and changed the course of mine forever. *What is the "chance" of that?*

A picture is worth a thousand words.

My shock and preoccupation over my father's cancer diagnosis caused me to overlook one very precious detail carefully placed at

Chapter 9: Jump at the Chance

the very end of his letter; he had struggled in how he should have signed it, and he tenderly chose, "Love, Dad." After our first several phone calls, I was ready to "take our relationship to the next level," so to speak, and I asked if he was comfortable with me calling him "Dad."

"I would be honored, darlin', but I feel unworthy of such a title," he said.

Many things have been written about the difference between what makes a "father" and what makes a "dad." I recall a frequently cited quote, "Any man can become a father, but it takes someone special to be a dad." John had unknowingly become a father, but he was becoming a dad as a fully willing and intentional participant in our relationship.

Since I'd never seen photos of my biological mother before, I didn't know who I resembled more . . . An annoying little thought persisted that, up until then, the only real evidence of our shared heritage consisted of documents with both our names on them. What if the photos bore no family resemblance? Would that cause questions and doubts to form, and bring forth uncertainty for us both? Apprehensively, I reached into the envelope and pulled out a handful of carefully chosen photographs. My heart thumping, I slowly turned the pile over, and my eyes zeroed right in on the tall, silver-haired, ruggedly handsome man standing alongside his beautiful, amber-colored quarter horse gelding, Folly. I sat in awe, and all I could do was grin from ear to ear as I stared in total amazement. I looked exactly like this man! It was a dead ringer!

His steely-blue eyes had finally solved the mystery of where my youngest daughter got her big blue eyes. From his high cheekbones to his smile, every photo revealed overwhelming physical DNA evidence that, without a shadow of a doubt, this was my father!

You could have easily mistaken him for a movie actor of the past, in his circa-1950s black-and-white photos sporting blond, slicked-back hair, chiseled features, and cleft chin, a pseudo-"James Dean" type. The older, more recent photographs of him taken on the ranch were much more reminiscent of the "Marlboro Man." He was a cowboy—a rugged outdoorsman and another "fierce Leo" in my life. I'd never seen another adult with whom I shared even one physical attribute, so to gaze at a photograph of a complete stranger and see my reflection staring back at me was profoundly surreal.

I grabbed the phone and dialed his number without skipping a beat. I wanted to share my exuberant joy over our inordinately strong family resemblance, which left no doubt that I was his daughter! At the same time, trepidation took center stage concerning his cancer disclosure, and how to approach it. At first, I tripped over my words while trying to get past the "elephant in the room," but he intuitively said, "It's okay, hon, I'm not going anywhere." In response, I could only utter two words: "You promise?" He firmly replied, "I promise, honey. The doc says they can't find any cancer in me, and we found it immediately, which is very rare. It's going to be okay."

"Let me tell you about the day I found out I had cancer," he went on. "Kathy had planned an elaborate garden party with over a hundred guests to celebrate my retirement from the school district. Colleagues, international students, friends, family, and assorted guests came from near and far."

It was a day of great celebration to honor the impact my father had had on so many people's lives over his thirty-five-year career. He was filled with anticipation over all the new opportunities a long-awaited retirement would afford him.

He said, "In the middle of the party, my doctor called, so I excused myself and stepped inside, assuming it was just a routine call concerning the X-ray results from the fall I'd suffered on my horse a few months before. In actuality, the doctor told me that, although my ribs had healed perfectly, the X-rays also revealed

Chapter 9: Jump at the Chance

the early onset of lung cancer." With travel plans already in the works, and exciting new adventures just around the corner, John was instead handed a potential death sentence. He said, "I hung up the phone, walked out into the celebratory crowd, and put on my best 'smiling Jack.' That was a very dark day, but all things considered, finding out now I have a daughter and two grandchildren makes up for all of it."

Chapter 10

A Chance Meeting

You were a risk, a mystery, and the most certain thing I'd ever known.

—Beau Taplin

A few days later, John received my photos and called immediately, ecstatic (like a proud father), exclaiming, "No doubt about it, darlin', you're mine, all right!" My little girl's heart began to swell like a hot-air balloon. Although I had no reference to what my mother looked like, it was clear I bore an uncanny resemblance to my father. After a lengthy chat, providing him the backstory on all the photos I'd sent, he said, "I would like for us to search out your mother together and see if we can find her." That felt unsettling, since she had been the one to who put me up for adoption. However, my father still had friends who lived in the area where they'd attended high school together, and he'd already started asking around. I sensed he needed to find her for his own reasons, but the hope that I might have the chance to meet my birth mother had me both terrified and desperately hopeful. I owed her my very life, and regardless of the reasons she gave me away, I would always be indebted to her for that. Now that I am a mother myself, I have a much deeper understanding of the unimaginable sacrifice she made. I'm quite certain her Catholic faith had a significant bearing on her decision to go through with the pregnancy and put me up for adoption. Had she chosen a different path, I wouldn't be here . . . and neither would my daughters. For that reason alone, nothing could have been of greater impor-

The Secret Identity of Chance

tance than having the opportunity to look her deep in the eyes and say, "Thank you." On the other hand, her rejection could be crushing should she be unwilling to acknowledge me or disinterested in pursuing a relationship with me.

John's wife, Katherine, arrived home from Idaho and immediately called, ecstatic at the prospect of becoming a grandma. She pulled apart some of my dad's baby albums, planning to send photos of him at different stages of his life for him and me to compare. I got the distinct impression that out of the two of them, she managed all the "important details." I was quite nervous about her reaction to me showing up out of the blue after all this time, but she couldn't have been more gracious and enthusiastic. Once she finished speaking with me, she handed the phone over to my dad. He said, "Honey, Kath and I would like to invite you, your husband, and the girls to come up and visit at the end of the month. We picked out a nice hotel close to where we live, and we would like to put you up for the weekend." I was delirious at the thought! My husband had seen the photos and accepted the realization that this *was* my father—and our girls' biological grandfather. I think he was secretly rather intrigued by the whole thing, and he seemed to be warming up to the idea. Life had thrown many unexpected things my way, but nothing in my wheelhouse of experiences had prepared me for this. I was at last going to meet my biological father!

Over the coming days, I couldn't think of much else. We would be arriving up north the week before Halloween. Our youngest child was only fifteen months old at the time, and our older daughter was three and a half, so meeting a new set of grandparents didn't confuse them at all. (Just wait until they grow up, and I have to make them a "family flowchart" to follow! No. Seriously.) Katherine made good on her promise, and over the next few days, I received a package that contained a stack of photographs of my father from infancy to adulthood. If you lined up baby photos of

Chapter 10: A Chance Meeting

my father, myself, and my youngest daughter, all at the same age, you would not be able to tell them apart. It was utterly shocking.

Along with the photographs she sent me was a note attached to another letter, which said, "Marla, your dad is unlike anyone you will ever meet. I thought this interview may give you a deeper context into who your father is. Lora is a longtime family friend who at the time was getting her degree in psychology, and she asked your dad if she could interview him for a class assignment. You and your dad have a lot of time to make up for, and I think this, more than anything else, may give you some understanding of your father before you meet him."

I opened the envelope and enclosed was this letter:

Interview with John McKeown Trust and Free Air

John McKeown is an old friend of my family's. My mother worked with his wife for over twenty years in the Berkeley School District. But it is not until recently that I have really connected with John. Five years ago, John was diagnosed with lung cancer. Against all odds, he is still alive. At one of my parents' parties, John and I got to talking about psychology, and he mentioned some interesting books and techniques he has been influenced by in his practice as a counselor in the Berkeley School District for over 35 years. We also got to talking of his work with horses, and of my fear of horses, and how one might see similarities in dealing with troubled children and horses. John invited me to take advantage of whatever resources he could offer me, so I chose John for this interview.

It was a rainy afternoon out at the ranch, and we sat in John's green SUV, discussing his career, thoughts, and experiences, as the windows fogged over the view of the old barn, the donkeys and the horses out to pasture in the Briones Valley. John described his work with children as that of an advocate. His job was to make sure they

89

were protected. When asked what quality was most important for a therapist to have when working with children, he responded: trust-worthiness. He explained that being trustworthy was a quality that grew with time, and one had to be open and committed to self-reflection in order to develop this quality, in order to become a good child psychologist. He said that kids are like horses, and any other living thing for that matter: they need to know you are trustworthy before you can develop any significant and healing relationship with them. How smart you are, and how well trained you are, both come second to this primary quality.

John's life has been significantly shaped by his passion for horses. His grandparents were ranch people; his grandmother never owned a car and till her dying day would take a horse to town.

Growing up, he said no one could keep him away from the horses. In his adulthood, he had the special luck of befriending Tom Dorrance, now popularly known as the "horse whisperer." John explained that Tom was a healer and would heal anything that came in his path, including John. Tom first noticed John because of his relationship with his horse, Folly. Folly was a wild horse that would buck every rider off to the ground. However, she had gotten very sick and had terrible open sores opening up along her chest and moving up to her throat. John took care of her. Twice a day he would scoot between her legs, under her body, and doctor her sores until they worked themselves up her chest, throat, and mouth, and finally out of her system. The whole process took about six weeks. After that experience, Folly trusted John, and would let him ride her, and even hide behind him for protection when she got frightened. Because of the relationship John fostered with Folly, Tom asked them to be his models for his "Natural Horsemanship" workshop. In these workshops, Tom taught that one never "broke" a horse; you just gained their trust to the extent that they chose to obey you.

When giving a directive to a horse, you gently nudge them in the right direction, and then free up the space so they can "move into free

Chapter 10: A Chance Meeting

air." This seems to have shaped John's approach to child therapy the most. He developed the ability to be nonjudgmental, and to let kids choose to be with him because he was safe, trustworthy, and knew how to help them. John also praises his longtime professor, mentor, and friend Harry Aaron, who kept encouraging him to study during his undergraduate and graduate work at Sacramento State, despite John leading a pretty rough-and-tumble life at the time. John's life experiences forced him to develop his toughness and street smarts, which he had to use to protect himself growing up, and which I am sure made his students and clients in the Berkeley School District both relate to him and feel protected by him. He also explained that this toughness came in handy when having to intimidate annoying colleagues into keeping their distance!

The biggest threat of burnout came from the people he called colleagues. He never got tired of his kids, but he did get tired of people who did not have a gift for being therapists, and therefore tried to make the art of therapy into a science in the hope of reducing it to quantifiable and controllable means. This was tiresome. It was also the reason John never became licensed. He could do his work easier without the restrictions of a license, and consequently having to jump through arbitrary hoops. Like the horses he loves, he refused to obey force and restriction. The greatest rewards of his work were to know that he had helped a kid. He continues to do so.

Road Trip

Map out your future-but do it in pencil. The road ahead is as long as you make it. Make it worth the trip.

—Jon Bon Jovi

It's a four-hundred-mile drive, and not much tests the patience of a parent more than the pitfalls of a long road trip with little ones

The Secret Identity of Chance

onboard. I didn't sleep a wink the previous night, as my phone rang off the hook with calls from well-wishers. I reminded myself that no matter what happened, it was a risk worth taking.

Once we were well on our way, the girls had fallen asleep, when I realized they were actually a much-needed distraction. Now it was just miles and miles of open road. Every green hundred-mile marker we crossed over getting us closer to our destination was like the last few jolts of an electric winch, winding up the hill of a colossal roller coaster as it prepared for the big drop. Tension was building in me the closer we got to our destination. I blankly stared at the cars slowly passing by, remembering the day I'd found my birth certificate when this uncertain journey began. I could have never imagined fate would fortuitously unfold the way it had, and in such a short amount of time. Never.

Collywobbles were burning in my stomach as the freeway turnoff was just two miles ahead. Soon we had pulled up to the hotel to freshen up and let the girls release some much-needed energy before we headed over to John and Katherine's house. I grabbed the bag of gifts I had packed for my dad and his wife, along with a large bag of green apples for his beloved Vito. We were ten minutes away when I felt all the blood rush to my head, and I began anxiously second-guessing whether this was a good idea or not. As we made our way through the quaint little town, I could taste a hint of blood, feeling the pain of broken skin on my bottom lip. I said, "Please drive slowly." I peered out the window, taken in by the charm of the neighborhood. Almost every house on the street was different from the next, quite a contrast to the big-development track homes I was more accustomed to. The tree-lined street was ablaze with golden rustic colors, and leaf-strewn lawns were artfully decorated for fall and Halloween. Gently cracked sidewalks lined both sides of the street, and each home proudly displayed hay bales, scarecrows, and carved pumpkins perched upon the old-fashioned porch steps, reminiscent of a long time

Chapter 10: A Chance Meeting

ago. As we slowly rolled up to my father's house, tidal waves of fear crashed over me, and I felt pulled beneath the whitewash of emotional terror. What if this didn't go well? What if he didn't approve of me? What if the tender connection we'd made over the phone felt completely different in person?

We stopped in front of their house with its perfectly manicured lawn, meticulously pruned shrubs, and a towering Japanese maple tree with burnt-orange and yellow leaves falling in the gentle autumn breeze. A tall, silver-haired gentleman with a full mustache stood in the driveway, leaning against a green SUV. He was alone. Once he spotted us, he yelled to Katherine in the house that we'd arrived. Within seconds, she bounded out of the house and down the steps with outstretched arms.

She was petite, stylish, and had the most delicate, soft blue eyes. My little girls jumped out of the car and ran to their new "grandma," as she knelt down in joyous laughter and enveloped them in enduring bearhugs. Then they turned and ran to their "grandpa," tightly wrapping their little arms around his legs, not wanting to let go. He struggled to gain his composure. I had already explained to my girls that these were their grandparents, so they instinctively knew they would be loved.

Katherine introduced herself first, then gave us a quick hug and took everyone inside to get acquainted, leaving my dad and me outside alone. I assumed my father had arranged this ahead of time as a way to create a safe space for us to have a few private emotional moments together. I nervously stayed behind, but then found myself standing alone on the other side of the lawn. The crisp fall breeze blew through my hair while the smoky aroma of a lit fireplace somewhere close by momentarily distracted me from the awkwardness of the moment. He was dressed in Levi's, a stone-washed-denim button-up shirt, well-worn brown leather cowboy boots, and a brown leather belt cinched in the middle with a large, intricately designed solid-silver belt buckle with the letters *JSM* centered and monogrammed in gold. He was still leaning against his SUV wearing sunglasses perched right above the silver walrus mustache that characterized his face and drooped over his top lip. I hesitantly made my way over to him.

Talking over the phone had felt much safer. He carried himself in a formidable manner, and if I hadn't known he was my father, I might have been intimidated to approach him. I stood frozen, until he smiled and motioned me over. I walked up to him, my heart laid bare, words stuck in my throat. I stood directly in front of him, trembling, as I tried to force an awkward smile, in awe that our resemblance in person was more striking than in the photos. We instantly locked eyes, like warriors who against all odds had taken in a great victory that day, conquering every conceivable obstacle, and at last had found each other. He reached out with open arms, and I recognized the familiar, woodsy scent that smelled just like the first letter he'd sent to me. Soon the tension began to release and dissolve into uncontrollable tears as I thought how remarkable it was that we had unknowingly existed on two sides of a vast ocean—oceans of distance, circumstance, and impossibility that seemed meant to keep us separated forever. I marveled at each miraculous and flawlessly placed stepping-stone laid in perfect synchronicity from the moment of my birth, that seemingly called us to cross over and brought us together.

Lockjawed, I literally couldn't speak. A paternal protectiveness emanated from him, unlike anything I had ever experienced as a child. I exhaled, for the first time feeling an absence of anxiety and freedom from doubt. The profound sacredness of this father-daughter moment had rendered us both unable to speak. Like a little girl in the arms of a loving, protective father, I started to cry—and he let me, as if he instinctively understood all the reasons why.

Chapter 10: A Chance Meeting

Life takes you unexpected places; love brings you home.

Katherine had taken the first possible opportunity to establish that she would be the "fun grandma," having set up Candy Land and Chutes and Ladders on the living room floor for her and the girls to play.

There was a large redbrick fireplace in the main room ablaze with fragrant cedar logs, which warmed the room and filled the air. As I walked in the front door, I immediately noticed that just above the black upright piano, a large frame proudly displayed a professional portrait of my dad and his wife in formal Western wear. My dad was sporting a sharp-looking white Stetson and his finest turquoise bolo tie. "What was the occasion for this portrait?" I asked.

"My dear friend and mentor, Tom Dorrance—the 'horse whisperer'—was the winner of the Chester A. Reynolds Award, established in 1990 in honor of the National Cowboy and Western Heritage Museum's founder. This photo was taken when Tom was recognized as a person whose lifestyle represents the ideals of the American West, and in 1995 he was inducted into the National Cowboy Hall of Fame. He asked me to be his honorary guest that evening." My father stood a little taller retelling this story, immensely proud of his dear friend and mentor.

Polished mahogany hardwood floors ran throughout the house, with colorful hand-knotted wool carpets from around the world strategically placed from one end to the other. A stunning antique China hutch sat in the formal dining room, a prize possession my father had inherited from his mother. My adrenaline rush began to slowly calm, as the savory smell of dinner cooking lingered in the air while Katherine finished setting a beautiful table for us with her favorite PortMeirion, Botanical Garden China. My dad offered to give me a quick tour of the charming one-story home

The Secret Identity of Chance

where they had lived all their married life. In his den sat an oversized, dark leather recliner covered in genuine bearskin, and a giant photograph of a lion's head hung on the wall. There was only one other thing that hung on the adjacent wall: a poem beautifully etched in black-and-white calligraphy, encased in a simple black wooden frame. I asked, "What is this?" and John replied, "I had this hanging in my office my entire career—these are the fundamental principles I have built my life on."

These are the words of the poem:

As honest words may not sound fine, Fine words may not be honest ones; A good man does not argue, and an arguer may not be good! The knowers are not learned men, And the learned men may never know. The Wise Man does not hoard his things; Hard pressed from serving other men, He has enough and some to spare; But having given all he had, He then is very rich indeed. God's Way is gain that works no harm; The Wise Man's way is to do his work without contending for a crown.

John walked me over to an antique console, where he proudly pulled out a wooden drawer that revealed his treasured Scottish knife collection. They were beautifully handcrafted, intricate, and most intimidating. I got the distinct impression that if push came to shove, he was masterfully skilled in how to use them.

I felt the warmth of the fireplace on my cheeks as we made our way back into the living room. I couldn't take my eyes off my father. I studied each facial expression, surprised at the many ways they were similar to mine, along with so many other things: the way he burst out in laughter telling his own stories; the way he'd slowly cross one long leg over the other; his trademark high cheekbones

Chapter 10: A Chance Meeting

(something I've always taken for granted); his observant and serious mannerisms when assessing a situation; and his unparalleled memory for detail. From the time I was very young, I'd developed the ability to "read a room" and pick up on emotional cues almost immediately. I've often been told that I had a certain peculiarity for memory and detail that was uncommon; my father had the exact same bent. Similarly, we don't care much for idle chitchat or small talk. He infused intentionality and meaning into the words he chose.

When I speak to a person, I want to "see" what they may not be saying with mere words, and I was intrigued that my father peered into the hearts of people when he spoke, in search of the same. I silently studied his every move from across the room, as shock continued to render me tongue-tied. I flashed back to the interview I'd read at the beginning of this journey, of the actor who had recounted his first emotional encounter with his biological father in a Scottish pub.

Something about that story had gripped me and resonated with me, in such a strange, unexplainable way; and similarly, here I sat, months later, with my own Scottish father sitting across the room as I listened to him tell stories of his life and adventures. I found myself so overwrought with emotion I was unable to speak. It was uncanny—although thousands of people might have breezed right through that article without giving it another thought, I saw the raw reflection of myself in that actor's story. Is that why it evoked such unrest in my soul, and why it had such a perplexing effect on me? Is it conceivable that his story was a type of "foreshadowing" of my own similar story, yet to be revealed? *What's the "chance" of that?*

The Secret Identity of Chance

Because every picture tells a story...

There were several old photo albums strategically placed on a rustic wooden trunk that served as a coffee table sitting in the middle of the room. John asked, "Would you like to go through some family albums together?" Still trying to comprehend the fact that my flesh-and-blood father was literally sitting across the room from me seemed more than I could handle in that moment, let alone absorb an entire family album, but I was thrilled at the notion, and my anxious curiosity overshadowed my hesitation. I timidly sat next to him, and he said, "Are you doin' okay, honey? I know this is a lot to take in."

Nervously twisting my hair around my index finger, I replied, "It's all right, Dad. I'm okay." I felt some measure of comfort knowing that he understood the gravity this held for me. He picked up a red Florentine leather album with gold piping around the edges. Although it had been well cared for, its color had faded through time, and the cracked leather showed its age. John handed it to me, displaying an endearing eagerness to bring me into the "family clan." This father-daughter moment was a "rite of passage." Oddly, I should have felt equally as excited, but I was actually very torn inside. I felt deeply conflicted; as if opening those mysterious pages was somehow an act of disloyalty to the only family I'd loved and known all my life. And yet, this was also my family—my family of origin. Remembering that my loved ones had sent me off with their blessing made it a bit easier, but I couldn't help but wonder if it would ultimately change me, to the point that I could never go back.

Grandchildren are the dots that connect the lines
from generation to generation.

—Lois Wyse

Chapter 10: A Chance Meeting

Opening the fragile leather cover, I first laid eyes on my biological grandfather. At first glance, I didn't see any particularly striking resemblance to him, or he to my father, for that matter. It surprised me. I guess for some reason, I'd expected him to look exactly like my dad. In the old black-and-white photos, he appeared studious, yet meek and mild. He had a rather tall forehead and a pointed chin with round, horn-rimmed spectacles that rested perfectly on his heart-shaped face. He was tall, thin, and dapper in an old-fashioned kind of way, with a meticulously trimmed and manicured mustache. I noticed that in almost every photo, he wore a pristine, nicely pressed white collared, button-up shirt and tie, but he was mostly in a full suit, vest, an appropriately placed pocket square, and a gold pocket watch, which hung from his waistcoat pocket. It was quite a contrast to the grandpa I had grown up with, who was a mason by trade. He was an honorable, hardworking union man, but I don't think he ever owned a suit, let alone a pocket square.

Grandparents love you in an unconditional way that's distinctly different from anyone else. The reality hit me that I would never know this man in the suit, my grandfather. I stared at his gentle face and felt such a longing to connect with him. I wished I could have reached through space and time and yelled, "Here I am, Grandpa, here I am!" But I missed him. I was the only grandchild born from his only son, and I would imagine that alone would have paved the way for a very special relationship. My heart was heavy that I would never know him. As I turned the pages, trying to avoid the lump in my throat, I imagined what kind of grandpa he would have been had I grown up with my father. As my dad picked up on the change in my countenance, he put his arm around me and said, "Would you like me to tell you a little about your grandparents?" I nodded my head, and he leaned back against the couch, crossing his legs and exposing his impeccably polished leather cowboy boots. Taking a deep breath, he stared off into space for what seemed like minutes. Then, he began to give me context to my lineage, explaining in colorful detail some of the interesting characters who made up my ancestral heritage.

My dad said, "My father came from a close and loving family. When he was ten years old, his mother contracted tuberculosis, and the family moved to Fort Collins, Colorado, establishing a home on a fifty-acre ranch." I was connecting the dots; "ranch life" was in my father's bloodline from the very start, although such ambitions had eluded my grandfather.

"What was his profession?" I asked.

He replied, "My father started out as a scientific assistant, in the U.S. Bureau of Entomology, and later became a superintendent of schools, a high school principal, a science teacher, and a clinical psychologist. He ended his career as the district educational advisor for Sacramento." I saw beautiful golden threads woven between my father and my grandfather. They had both spent the entirety of their professional lives in education, helping the vulnerable and advocating for children.

A Safe Place for Faith

There was a subtle shift in my dad's voice when he spoke of his father, almost a twinge of regret. Turning the page, he stopped at a particular photograph in which my grandfather was standing in a church setting, and my dad became very quiet, reflective... almost uncomfortable. He silently got up and slowly walked across the room, tossing a few cedar logs onto the dwindling flames.

Still with his back turned toward me, poking at the fire, he cautiously began to speak, saying, "I want to give you some context into the faith of your grandfather, because I think it will be meaningful for you, Marla. While in his college years, he became a Christian, and he was all his life thereafter, an active member of the Presbyterian Church. In Fort Collins, as a young man he was

Chapter 10: A Chance Meeting

an elder in his home church, and for some years he was the superintendent of the Sunday school. He was an elder in the Presbyterian Church of Sacramento during his active years there, and in the early period, while living in Alameda, he supervised a college-age young people's group in the church he attended with my mother."

I replied, "So, like me, you must have also grown up in the church?"

My dad responded, letting out a huge belly laugh with a dose of humorous sarcasm. "Yep, the church of the gray hairs," he said, breaking the awkwardness of the moment. "His faith was deeply sacred to him, and not just 'religious practice.'"

I'd concluded, from things my father had mentioned in previous conversations, that he had been deeply hurt and disappointed by religious people growing up. Most of us have. However, he grew up watching his father live out his faith in sincere humility, which might have been why my father remained a truth seeker his entire life. However, his truth may have looked different than his father's growing up in Berkeley in the sixties, as it was a time of nonconformity from the establishment, and, like many other young people of the time, he challenged the status quo and made up his own mind about what he wanted to believe. I would imagine this could have been a source of tension between a father and son. Tilting his head back, my dad exhaled slowly, smoothing his mustache with his thumb and forefingers. "But I always knew my dad loved me dearly."

Holding his intense stare, I smiled back, saying, "Well, Dad, I guess Grandpa and I share something very special in common, then."

He squeezed my hand and touted, "There's one more thing I know for sure—he would have absolutely adored you, darlin'." My father cautiously cracked open a door to an extremely vulnerable place, allowing me to follow. He was an immensely private man,

The Secret Identity of Chance

and this level of exposure was not something he offered to many. I felt the weight of such a sacred trust.

Although I've held on to the faith I grew up with, and I've made my peace with some of the unanswerable questions of the universe, I understood that my father was, in many ways, still searching. Sadly, however, in the spring of 1958, a terrible mishap befell his father. My grandfather lost his balance and plummeted from a tall ladder, striking his head on the driveway. He endured a serious head injury that required two massive brain surgeries within weeks of the fall. He was hospitalized for over seven weeks, and although he was not paralyzed, the left side of his brain was permanently damaged, and it affected his speech and ability to conjure (aphasia). At the time of the accident, he had been a psychologist, but he had to retire from active professional life as a result of his injuries.

Eventually Grandpa recovered from the fall, but sadly, my dad said, "he was never quite the same." My dad loved his father, but the changes in some of his behaviors after the accident were confusing and hard for him to understand as a youth; it often drew a wedge between them. Dad became somber as he reflected, "It was only after I entered the university, and had the opportunity to study psychology and different aspects of the brain, that I realized that much of the conflicts I had with my father were due to the physiological injuries he sustained, over which he had absolutely no control." I sensed deep regret in my father's voice, as his tone softened to tender endearment, and he said, "It can truthfully be said of my dad that his whole life was spent in educational interests and enterprises, and all his adult years in helping young people to find their place in the scheme of things . . . he was a very sweet man."

Legacies of servant-leadership were woven between my dad and my grandfather, as they had both spent the entirety of their professional lives in education, helping the vulnerable and

Chapter 10: A Chance Meeting

advocating for children. And although working with children was not my professional vocation, I've spent most my life passionately volunteering in a broad range of youth programs. I've always had a deep love for mentoring and counseling young people, and this devoted "calling" has followed me well into adulthood. Nobody ever modeled this for me growing up; it was innate. Something inside me always gravitated toward helping kids.

Perhaps my father and grandfather's DNA had been intrinsically imprinted on me from the very beginning.

Lucille

The photo of a slim, fair skinned woman with a full head of magnificently coiffed silver hair looking quite sophisticated in her blush pink–rimmed cat's-eye glasses caught my attention, and my dad remarked, "Your grandmother Lucille was not only a total extrovert, but quite a pistol." Her physical resemblance and facial symmetry was strikingly similar to that of both my father and me. I couldn't help but wonder if that was what I would look like at her age. In every photo, she was impeccably dressed down to her shoes, brooch, and matching pearl earrings. She held the same fixating gaze as my father, like they could see right through you. She carried herself in a dignified and refined manner. My dad leaned in and recounted, "She came from nothing—after her father was killed in a mill accident and her mother and many siblings were cast into abject poverty—but she was determined to be an educated and refined person, and she worked hard at it. She was a confident woman who could—and wanted to—command a room. She was a hoot, but you wouldn't want to cross her. She was quite a formidable woman." The inflection of his tone shifted to endearing respect and surprising humor in regard to the tenacity and fortitude of his strong-willed mother; she, unlike most, was an equal match for him. He leaned in and said, "Well, hon, where do I

The Secret Identity of Chance

even begin with your grandmother?" He slapped his leg and broke out in a bellow of laughter. "Your grandmother was extremely well read, and she knew just about everything there was to know on any given subject. She read every book there was worth reading and devoured the *New York Times* cover to cover every day of her life. After she and my father married, they left Oregon and made their way to Northern California, where they remained, and they raised my two older sisters and me. She worked in administrations in the governor's office in Sacramento for her entire career, under four governors—Goodwin J. Knight, Edmund G. Brown Sr., and Ronald Reagan, in addition to Earl Warren before he was appointed chief justice of the U.S. Supreme Court by President Eisenhower."

Letting off a half-suppressed laugh, he said, "One of your grandmother's most intriguing—and annoying—characteristics was her uncanny ability to extract private details from a person before they even knew what was happening. Those who knew her well often said she should have worked for the FBI because she could get information out of anyone. This was often a pain in my neck, especially in my rebellious youth, when my mother instinctively knew I was up to something and would 'innocently' interrogate my friends. Inevitably they would end up 'spilling their guts' without fail.

"She was very shrewd, and she had a rather well-developed sense of mischief. Gotta like that in a person. She ended up developing scarlet fever in the first few years after she was married. Apparently, it causes your hair to fall out, and my mother got tired of hunks of the stuff just coming out randomly, so she shaved her head. She was quite pleased with herself. She put a cap on, and when my father came home from work, she whipped it off merrily to show him her totally bald head. My dad was a squeamish kind of guy, and he was a bit horrified. Even fifty years later, my mom seemed rather indignant!"

Chapter 10: A Chance Meeting

My father was her only son, and the "apple of her eye," and perhaps they were more alike than either of them cared to admit. Growing up, I had always longed for a strong woman like my grandmother Lucile to aspire to. Might it be possible that the essence of this courageous forebearer who shared my DNA had been growing up on the inside of me all along?

The Aunties

My dad's mood shifted as he began to reminisce over the life of his youngest sister, Dorothy, whom he was very close to growing up. He spoke softly. "She was a stunning blond-haired, blue-eyed beauty. In the early war years, she fell head over heels in love with an Air Force officer whom she met at a USO dance, named Richard. They were married just before he went overseas.

"Richard's plane was shot down, and he was killed a few months after they were married."

Although my father was quite young when Richard's plane was shot down, his brother-in-law made an indelible mark on my dad as a little boy. He was a type of "war hero" in my father's life. The reverence that settled in the space between us while he spoke of Richard was palpable.

"Dorothy ended up going back to the university and became an occupational therapist, and she was working at that after the war when she met a wonderful man, who was just finishing his PhD in psychology at Stanford. They married and had two sons, both very successful in their prospective careers. Sadly, my sister became very ill, and she died prematurely of health-related issues." His soft voice muddled into somber introspection as he gently turned the page.

Both sisters were considerably older than my father when he was born, but the eldest, Florence, was still alive, and married to the love of her life. The weathered pages were filled with pho-

The Secret Identity of Chance

tographs of this distinguished couple and their travels all over the world, in scenes that looked "ceremoniously official." She was a tall, thin, fresh-faced brunette, very stylish, reminiscent of an early Ingrid Bergman. She held herself in refined elegance, much like my grandmother Lucille. "My sister Florence studied journalism and then economics at UC Berkeley. Shortly before she would have graduated, she took the train to Boston to marry a Cal alumnus and newly commissioned submarine officer," Dad explained as he pointed to a handsome, debonair young man in military uniform. "That's your uncle Bill. After World War II, Bill entered the U.S. Foreign Service, which took them all over the world, from Stockholm to Malawi. They had four children, all very successful. Eventually, they ended up in Rome, where they lived before retiring to Berkeley. She and Bill fell in love with Italy, and all things Italian. They were wonderful cooks, and she was known for her porcini stuffing at Thanksgiving, and Neapolitan patisserie. Since my mother's passing, Florence has been the keeper of the family stories, as you will soon find out. Your uncle Bill is a retired State Department and U.N. diplomat. He and my sister had quite the glamorous life living abroad, and Mother's favorite thing was when they would come back to the States to visit and tell of all their adventures. There was always a lot of fussing at my house when Florence and Bill came to town.

"Your uncle Bill spent more than thirty-five years as a diplomat, first with the U.S. State Department and then with the United Nations. Among his postings were as the U.S. consul general in Florence, Italy, and the director of the U.N.'s World Food Program in Pakistan. He and Florence both had a knack for languages and a deep knowledge of foreign policy. And nobody threw a more elegant dinner party than my sister. After Bill retired from the State Department and the U.N., he and my sister settled in the Berkeley hills, right up the street from where I live."

Chapter 10: A Chance Meeting

Biting off the last bit of the tip of my thumbnail, I said, "Wow, that's a lot to take in." My countenance fell as I realized I didn't have impressive academic degrees, and I had never held a political office—or even lived abroad, for that matter. I was not feeling confident in my ability to "fit in" with my newfound family. Looking at my dad, I said, "I think I may be quite nervous meeting them."

He smiled and said, "Hon, there is nothing to be afraid of. It was his personality that made your uncle Bill such a great diplomat. He is very gracious, kind, and well-mannered, and he knows how to make everyone in the room feel comfortable. And by the way, darlin', the entire family is dying to meet you and the girls on your next trip up."

My grumbling stomach started vying for my attention just as Katherine called us in for dinner. My senses were overloaded as my imagination labored to color in all the blank spaces left from my father's fascinating family history lesson. These captivating and colorful characters were "my people," but in glaring contrast, I kept coming back to the fact that there was nothing particularly riveting about me. My fork twirled around my pasta as I scooted the vegetables from one side of my plate to the other, and my voracious appetite gave way to the unnerving distractions in my head.

Over dinner, my dad mentioned our lineage as Mayflower descendants, as well as Daughters of the American Revolution. He said, "My mother and her side of the family kept impeccable family records. It has taken years to compile all the family history, obtain verified authentications of the family line-carrier, and gather the notarized acceptance letters from both societies . . . and I'm sure my sister is working on providing all of that for you and the girls as we speak! Our family also has a very interesting lineage tracing back to France, but I think you've had enough for tonight, and I don't want to overwhelm you, dear."

107

The Secret Identity of Chance

I was pretty certain that ship had already sailed!

What's Real

Katherine made coffee while I put the last of the clean dishes away. Out the corner of my eye, I noticed my father in the next room with his newly found granddaughters curled up on each knee. He was reading to them from the assortment of children's books he and Katherine had purchased especially for our visit. My mind drifted back to an experience, albeit a polar opposite one, I'd had with a grandparent when I was very young.

While my parents took a rare weekend trip away, my three younger brothers and I were left at home to be watched over by our grandmother. Although she was the biological grandmother to two of my three brothers, I never had reason to believe that I was anything less than her granddaughter. She was old-school, rough around the edges, very strict, and orderly, and she ran her day pursuant to stringent schedules and routines.

Anyone with three little boys ranging a year apart in age knows that trying to keep "everything and everyone" on a strict regimen is nearly impossible in that situation. Our home growing up was controlled chaos, but chaos just the same. It didn't take long for my grandmother to become indignant over the fact that my hyperactive little brothers were not immediately responding to her many instructions.

Respectfully, I tried to offer a few foolproof suggestions that worked every time. Shockingly, what I received in response was a harsh and angry rebuke: "I don't need you to tell me what to do with my own grandchildren; you and Kevin [my adopted brother] are not my real grandchildren, so I do not need any help from you!"

I never heard scary words like those in my home, and I was thankful Kevin was not around to hear it. I had always loved my grandmother, and I never knew this was how she truly felt about

108

Chapter 10: A Chance Meeting

me. Filled with shame, I recoiled to my bedroom and cried myself to sleep that night. I dared not make another sound for the rest of the weekend until my parents arrived home. Of course, I told my parents what happened, and they were swift to try to rectify the situation, but sadly, the damage was done. Those crushing words filled my young mind with confusion and singed my emotional skin. Once again I was left to struggle with what "real" meant, and what my identity was (or wasn't) in relation to that. I would have given anything to have had what my daughters were experiencing with their biological grandfather, and if this was the only thing I walked away from this experience with, it would have all been worth it.

Wrapping things up for the night, we went over plans for the following day; my dad was eager to get an early start. We were going to meet, and ride, his beloved Vito. Inviting us into his private sanctuary was important to him, and he did not extend such an invitation to just anyone. I hoped this experience would give me a much deeper insight into the complexities of this intriguing man—who was my father.

As I hugged him at the front door while getting ready to leave, I noticed the makeup smudges from my tear-stained face still left upon his denim shirt, and I remembered how terrified I had been only hours before.

We said our good-byes, and I snuck in one last hug and said, "I love you, Dad."

He enveloped me in a bear hug, smiling from ear to ear, and said, "I love you, too, darlin'. I'm so glad you're here." There have been many memorable days that changed the course of my life, but this day I will remember forever.

A Tiny Little Star

Sitting down on the grassy lawn outside our hotel room door, exhausted by the emotional gravity of the day, I wrapped myself in a warm blanket and stared up at the brilliant stars filling the autumn sky. This remarkable journey felt like a divine gift—like God had broken all the rules for me. He cleared a path for my dad and me, where there was no path. I can't help but wonder why, out of all the years I could have stumbled upon my original birth certificate, why now? What would my life have looked like had I found him sooner? I've always held on to the belief that, being given away, I was simply lucky to have beaten the odds and made it out alive; that children like me didn't grow up and hold a definitive place of destiny, because that was a birthright reserved for those who were "chosen." This narrative was my framework. Now, looking at it from "Mount Perspective," perhaps luck had nothing to do with it. Maybe . . . I was *"born on purpose."* Like the galaxy of stars seated in the heavens above me, this "family reunion" felt like I had been joined together with something much bigger than myself. In contrast to the magnificent constellations, I am

Chapter 10: A Chance Meeting

just one, tiny little star, in the vast hemisphere of ancestral lineage which has gone before me. They have shifted and moved to make space for me, and I now hold a place alongside them. Like the stars, I have become part of their cluster, and we are bigger and brighter together.

Chapter 11

Chance of a Lifetime

Coyote Ridge Ranch

Bleary-eyed and bone tired, I rolled out of bed after a night of constant tossing and turning as my mind labored through the night trying to reset to a place of normalcy: from before I arrived here. A place that no longer existed. We pulled up to the house shortly after the sun came up, where my father stood alone waiting for us, blue-jeaned in his classic Wranglers, cowboy boots, and a snappy white Stetson, perfectly placed and tilted just above his brow.

Quickly piling out of the car, the girls raced across the lawn (in a straight beeline toward him), screaming, "Grandpa, Grandpa!" He bent down and wrapped them in his arms like purring kittens. The expression of exuberant joy on his face could only be matched by the look of sheer disbelief. The comforting aroma of coffee brewing and sticky buns in the oven was a warm greeting as we stepped through the front door. We gobbled down breakfast, knowing Dad was anxious to get going. I climbed up into his big green Denali, while the distinctive smells of a horse stable permeated the air. The back seat was loaded with riding saddles and colorful Mexican wool saddle blankets. The worn leather saddles gave off a strong earthy, slightly sweet aroma that took my imagination to the prairies of the Old West.

The Secret Identity of Chance

 The peaceful drive carried us up and down scenic mountain hills on a single-lane country road. He would only drive the back way, and though it took a little longer, a quicker route was never an option. I watched a metamorphosis take over as he steered through the steep incline and gradual descent of winding, tree-lined roads, edging our way closer to the ranch, as his countenance became calm and relaxed. He said, "We could take the freeway and get there a lot faster, but getting somewhere faster doesn't mean better. Everyone is in a big hurry to get nowhere as fast as they can." Gazing out the window, I pondered over that statement as it pertained to my own life. How often I am running on fumes, rushing about in the constant busyness of life feeling like I'm on autopilot simply jetting from one task to another, rarely taking the opportunity to stop and take a breath.
 My shoulders untightened as we weaved through the outskirts of Briones Regional Park with mile after mile of rolling hills and oak-dotted grasslands. Once we turned off the main road, it opened to breathtaking panoramic views in every direction. "It's not uncommon to see lots of wildlife out here, besides cows and calves grazing. There's black-tailed deer, coyotes, squirrels, red-tailed hawks, and turkey vultures . . . not to mention, the seasonal wildflowers are really somethin' to behold. This is where I come to escape." Since retiring, this was where you would find him on any given day. The quiet, undisturbed natural beauty of this idyllic paradise is much more to him than just a peaceful des-

Chapter 11: Chance of a Lifetime

tination. The ranching lifestyle is in his blood, and this is where he feels truly alive, the most authentic version of himself.

Although he spent the entirety of his professional career in a shirt and tie, he is without question an "all-American cowboy" at heart. There's an unbridled sense of joy spilling out of him as he relays stories of his life on the ranch, but deep down, he is like a wild stallion, just on the brink of breaking down the corral and running free at any attempt to "break" him.

Curious about the contrast between my father's passion for ranching and that of his older sister, who spent most her adult life traveling abroad and living what one might consider an "upper crust" life as the wife of a U.S. diplomat, I asked him if his sister had ever aspired to any aspect of ranch life. I had barely finished my sentence, when he burst out in laughter! "The love of horses and ranch life was some kind of genetic imprinting that completely missed my sister altogether. It seemed to have only affected me and my sister Dorothy's two adult sons. They both ended up in Colorado, where their lives, outside of work, were dominated by horses."

I wondered whether the name "Vito" had some deep sentimentality, and I asked, "Dad, why Vito?" He smiled and said, "Vito Corleone, from *The Godfather*. The best series ever made." Though I have never watched the movie in its entirety (only because I get a bit queasy over blood and guts), I am familiar with the iconic role Marlon Brando brilliantly portrayed. A man who lived by a strict moral code of loyalty, and above all, family. The name wasn't chosen due to sentimentality, but rather admiration.

Approaching Coyote Ridge Ranch, we passed by a charming ranch-style home with a wraparound porch and white picket fence. There were old wooden rocking chairs draped with knitted blankets sitting atop the porch steps, and seasonally decorated pumpkins, fall wreaths, and whimsical, hay-stuffed scarecrows

The Secret Identity of Chance

holding a WELCOME sign at the entrance. My dad told me, "That's where the owner of the property lives."

Passing by several smaller stables on each side of the dirt road, listening to the gravel popping beneath the tires, we made our way to the main stalls, where Vito was boarded. I stepped down to the sound of fallen oak leaves crunching under my feet, and the pungent smell of sweet hay and horse manure lingering in the air. I immediately found myself engulfed in a swarm of pesky horseflies. Nonchalantly, my father pulled out the saddles from the back of the truck while I observed his response (or lack thereof) to being attacked by hundreds of filthy, annoying insects; it didn't faze him at all. Following his lead, and determined to suck it up, I pretended it didn't bother me, either.

Several curious friends headed over after seeing my dad surrounded by an entourage, and he proudly introduced us. These were his "barn friends." They've built long-standing, trusted relationships around their passion for horses. Katherine leaned over and said, "It's not uncommon for these ladies to call your dad at all hours of the day or night when they need help with their horses and the vet isn't readily available." At that moment, I was occupying his world, and being introduced as his daughter felt like a tremendous honor.

He said, "Hon, will you grab the box from the back of the truck and bring it over?"

I carried the large cardboard box over to the horse trailer, and started to unload it, puzzled by the dozens of cans of cat food inside. I asked, "Dad, what's the cat food for?"

He replied, "Well, there's a stray cat I named Reno that lives on the ranch, and I've taken him in. It gets really cold in the winter, so I bought a cat bed and made a home for him in my horse trailer. I made a small door, so he can come in and be sheltered from the elements and safe from predators. I feed and take care of him."

Chapter 11: Chance of a Lifetime

The big gray cat heard my dad's voice and darted out of nowhere, purring and rubbing up against his ankles like a long-lost friend. As a child, I, too, was notorious for bringing home strays. They could have been kittens, baby birds, stray dogs—you name it. I would sneak them into the house and hide them in my bedroom (much to my parents' chagrin). Watching my dad tenderly hold this ramshackle barn cat brought back similar memories from my own childhood. I flashed back to a seventh-grade classroom, when I rescued (well, more like grabbed and ran off with) a litter of unwanted kittens from a heartless middle-school science teacher who was going to feed them to her python. An unfamiliar courage bubbled up in me that day, having realized that you must protect those that can't care for themselves.

Watching my dad tenderly safeguard his adopted stray, I realized the old adage, "the apple doesn't fall far from the tree," might hold some merit. We are rescuers.

Sibling Rivalry

Coyote Ridge Ranch felt like a million miles away from anything manufactured, or artificial. We loaded our arms with leads and saddles and headed over to the fenced area, where Vito was grazing. My father called me over to give me a proper introduction, but Vito was uninterested at best, as he grazed upon the green grass. He was soft and warm when I hugged his large, muscular neck, and I quickly sensed by his aloof manner that he was "sizing me up." Just then, I pulled out the bag of juicy green apples, which he reluctantly took from me. My father referred to Vito as "his boy." This gorgeous creature, and his mother before him, had been the sole recipients of my dad's love, adoration, protection, and absolute devotion since birth. My father's face beamed from ear to ear as he led our little clan through the ranch complex, proudly introducing "his family" to every person he bumped into along the way. We entered a large covered outdoor arena, where he saddled up Vito for my little girls to ride. Methodically he checked and rechecked the equipment. As terrified as I was to see my babies on top of such a humongous animal, I trusted my father. He gently lifted them on top of Vito one by one and took him by a lead. He slowly walked around the arena while I nervously walked alongside.

Vito was calm and well-behaved; he never so much as flinched with my little ones saddled upon his back. He instinctively knew to be as gentle as possible. After a few trips around the arena, to my girls' sheer delight, my dad ended their ride with a treat for Vito for a job well done. Then came my turn. I still felt an awkward sense that he was "staring me down" as I cautiously made my way to his left side. I stepped up on the mounting block and firmly slipped my foot securely into the leather stirrups. I jumped up and swung my right leg over his back and settled in the saddle. I gave him a good rub on the side of his neck and said, "Good boy, Vito," and he snorted almost indignantly, waited a minute, and then unabashedly "relieved himself." I couldn't help but think the timing of this was suspicious . . . perhaps even deliberate.

I carefully took the soft, well-worn leather reins in the palms of my hands. It was just me, Vito, and my dad standing in the center arena. I ever so softly nudged him forward, and in one split

Chapter 11: Chance of a Lifetime

second, he took off like a bucking bronco! Stunned, I grabbed the reins, stood up in the stirrups, and tried to settle him down. "Whoa, boy! Slow down! Easy, boy!" He started running faster as we headed straight for the wall in front of us. I started yelling, "Daddy, help! What's wrong with him!? Whoa, boy!" The slower I wanted him to go, the faster he went! I could hear my little girls screaming for me in the distance as Vito was ready to buck me off at any second, and I thought, *I am not going to die right here in front of my children.* I steadily pulled the reins to one side, trying to get him into a circle pattern in hopes of slowing him down and avoiding the wall. Fortunately, I'd had a little riding experience, and my instincts kicked in, but I was terrified!

My dad calmly walked into the center arena and gave Vito a firm command, and the horse immediately hit a full stop, and I did a quick dismount. I looked at my dad, threw my hands up in the air, and said, "What in the heck just happened!? He was as sweet and docile as could be with the girls, and then he snapped the minute I hopped on his back?"

My father started laughing as he pet Vito's backside and said to him in a particularly playful tone, "A little sibling rivalry there, huh, boy?" He then told me, "Vito is jealous of you, darlin'. He knows who you are."

Oddly, I felt him trying to rattle me from the minute we got acquainted. He watched me intently out of the corner of his eye as I walked alongside my father arm in arm on the way to the arena. Clearly, "my four-legged brother" was testing me to see what I was made of.

Horses are socially intelligent animals, and it was quite possible Vito had picked up on the deep connection between me and my father and felt threatened by it. This beautiful, russet-colored gelding was the "crown prince." I had spent the greater part of my life having to adapt to the threats of a constantly changing family dynamic, and one thing I'd learned is that everyone

The Secret Identity of Chance

(even animals) needs to feel loved, valued, and safe. This animal had never had to share my father's affections with anyone but Katherine. I approached this massive animal and stood alongside him at his shoulder, staying perfectly still. I slowly edged my way closer so I could look him dead in the eye. In a soft voice, I said something to him I had repeatedly said to my own family through years of potentially worrisome relational transitions: "I'm not a threat. I'm just one more person to love you." Although I do not profess to be Dr. Doolittle, I could swear he understood exactly what I said. He seemed agreeable, as I watched his long, beautifully bushy tail swing back and forth behind him, and he pawed the ground, giving me an amiable "snort." Progress.

Don't cry because it's over, smile because it happened.

—Dr. Seuss

Dirty, dusty, and hungry, I climbed into Dad's truck and we drove down the long dirt road into the sunset and headed for home. Curious, I turned to my dad and asked, "Dad, what exactly did you mean by 'Vito knows who I am'?"

He paused, then replied, "The thing is, hon, you're my girl, and although you may not have known what you were capable of when you sat in the saddle, you sure did once you jumped off . . . and so did Vito. He was testing you. Life will test you in much the same way. You're going to climb up upon some scary things, things that will seem much bigger than anything you can handle . . . but always remember who you are, darlin', and you'll find your way."

I was transfixed by the amber sunset casting its warm shadows from the towering treetops as I'm jolted back into reality by an occasional pothole in the old two-lane back country road.

Something troublesome began gnawing at me, but I couldn't put my finger on it. Then it suddenly hit me: we were leaving in the morning. This summoned a deeply painful struggle I've

Chapter 11: Chance of a Lifetime

carried my entire life with saying "good-bye." I'd been so caught up in joy, relishing every second with my father, that I forgot the clock was ticking, and my time was running out. The burning sensation rumbled in my stomach as I sat motionless. I turned my head away, attempting to hide my tears while I stared at my somber reflection in the passenger-side window. After a moment of awkward silence, my dad gently said, "What's the matter, hon?"

With my heart lurched all the way up into my throat, I couldn't get a word out. So many painful good-byes I'd struggled to overcome throughout the course of my life left me feeling pummeled, like I was sitting at the bottom of Niagara Falls besieged with memories of abandonment and final farewells that left me fragmented. Early the next morning, I would have to say the one thing I'd never been able to say without anguish, "Good-bye." This wondrous experience would be coming to an end. Orphan hearts generally live in two camps: those who never allow themselves close enough to get deeply wounded, and those who wear their heart on their sleeves and pay dearly for it.

It's pretty easy to guess which camp I live in. Although I've wrestled and won many wars on the battlefields of abandonment issues, this good-bye thing took me down every time, and it goes back as far as I can remember.

I was about six when my adoptive parents divorced, and my dad moved to another city. It was a confusing time, and I missed him terribly. I would cry for days after he left from a weekend visit. As his visits became less frequent, the good-byes and extended separation became much more painful and difficult. This was the beginning of a life shouldered upon the constant upheaval of parents and stepparents who married, divorced, and remarried. It became a revolving door of trusted relationships coming "and going." I've often wondered if these gripping feelings of detachment could have started at birth. Did being permanently separated from my biological mother set a longing within me as early on as infancy? Of course, I don't remember any of it, but who's to say?

He turned to me and said, "You're awfully quiet, darlin'. What's troubling you?"

After a few seconds, I whispered with embarrassment, "Well, I have to leave you tomorrow." My quivering voice barely squeaked the words out before I bowed my head and sank back down into the seat.

Grappling with the tightness in my throat, I explained, "I've always had trouble with good-byes." All my childhood triggers were firing on all cylinders—a little girl again having to detach and say good-bye to her daddy, not knowing when I would see him again. My adult mind knew this was not rational, but I couldn't talk myself out of it. I'd succumbed to deep feelings of loss and detachment most of my life in various relationships, and I'd simply learned how to maneuver around it, but I'd never found the courage to conquer it. My dad reached over and gently gave my knee a pat, saying in a strong and reassuring tone, "Hon, I promise you I'm not going anywhere."

The Journey Home

Restless, I got up early before anyone else awoke. Thankfully, there was a working coffeemaker in the hotel room, which allowed me some quiet moments to gather my thoughts over a hot cup of coffee while I watched the sunrise, and before my active little ones sprang out of bed. All I could think about was saying good-bye to my father so soon, feeling like we still had an entire lifetime to make up for. As we got closer to his house, my heart began racing, my hands felt cold and clammy, and I could feel the all-too-familiar separation anxiety building. Again, my dad was standing out front waiting for us. The girls jumped straight out of the car and into his arms, and I watched this strong, ruggedly stoic-looking

Chapter 11: Chance of a Lifetime

man melt into "grandpa," beaming from ear to ear. The girls headed into the house with my husband to say good-bye to Katherine, and I slowly walked over to my dad, where he was standing waiting for me. I wanted to be strong and fearless because my father was. Somewhere deep within my DNA, this strength had to reside, but I couldn't find it. Hiding behind my sunglasses, I made my way to him, and he opened his arms while I stood there with my face buried in his denim jacket, unable to speak or fight back the tears. All I could do was whisper, "Thank you . . . for everything." I was filled with gratitude for the love, kindness, and grace he had extended to me and my family. Meeting in person created a powerful connection that fused us together as father and daughter. It was inexplicable in every way.

The girls came out and said their final good-byes while I struggled to let go of my father and the childlike security I felt in his presence. With my family in the car waiting to leave, knowing this was the final good-bye, the tension was building, and I couldn't move. He finally said, "Honey, it's okay. I'm not going anywhere. I love you."

I hugged him one last time and replied, "I love you, too, Daddy." I kissed him on the cheek, then got in the car as I watched him stand there until we drove away and he was out of sight.

I'd never been the one who consistently won the contests or took home the blue ribbons, but this must be how it felt. I had stepped into a position of honorary identity. I couldn't have asked, or even imagined, that my initial journey to my biological father a few short months ago could have ended up so unbelievably life-changing.

Watching the street signs heading home, my mind drifted back to the drive into town just a few days before, when I'd strongly wondered whether I should turn back. Sadly, I have allowed many things in my life to paralyze me with fear and hold me back. Opportunities I missed because of the dreaded "what ifs," only to realize

The Secret Identity of Chance

that everything I feared never materialized. I allowed the voices of other people, the voices of the world, and the voices in my head to stop me. There is a phrase, coined by Seneca, that could not be more true: "We suffer more in imagination than in reality." As I've come to know and trust the "still, small voice" within me, which has guided me all my life, I am immensely grateful I listened to it this time. I couldn't help but feel there was something much more consequential in the timing of all this, and that perhaps God, in His mercy, had been directing my steps all along... but why now?

As we drove out of the city and onto the mountainous open road, with the girls fast asleep in the back seat, I was left with a deafening silence between my husband and me. My husband had enjoyed meeting my dad and his wife and the time we spent together, but he was closed off and distant. It led me to ponder questions my dad had asked me in private over the weekend: questions about my marriage, questions for which I didn't have a good answer.

Joy and sadness come by turns.

—Walker Percy

Walking through own my front door after arriving back home felt strange, like everything so beautifully recognizable and intimately familiar now seemed a little askew. There was an odd message on my phone machine from my dad, asking me to call him first thing in the morning; his tone left me with an uneasy feeling. The next morning, I called as soon as I got up. "Hi, Dad."

He answered, "Hi, hon, how was your drive home?" We had a few minutes of idle chitchat about the drive, but I sensed something troubling under the surface. There was a long pause of awkward silence, and he finally said, "Darlin', I don't know how to tell you this. You know I have been trying to locate your mother since you found me, and because she and I went to high school

Chapter 11: Chance of a Lifetime

together, we have some mutual acquaintances that go way back. I've been asking around in hopes to find her, but I just learned she died on September 16, 1997. She may be buried at St. Joseph's in Elk Grove, which is where her funeral was held, and where she lived at the time. I was able to obtain the address of one of her brothers, Ken. I think you should reach out to him, honey. He may be able to give you more information about your mother and her side of the family."

The phone in my hand felt like a twenty-pound weight. Like a slap across the face was the reality that I would never meet the courageous woman who had carried me within her womb or understand the insurmountable fears and uncertainties that surrounded her at the time of my birth. I'd always hoped that one day I would find her and she would answer all my questions. I've often wondered what kind of emotional conveyance took place between my mother and me in those final hours. The agonizing, heartfelt cries of a mother who wanted more for her child than the life she could provide, and the sacrificial relinquishment of all her maternal hopes and dreams for me. I was her protected secret. For nine emerging months, she was my mommy, and I was her baby girl. Her womb was a safe and sacred space, a place where I might have recognized the sound of her voice, felt her love and troubled emotions, and been lulled to sleep by the steady beating of her invincible heart. We were one. I never wanted to carry on without her, but just as giving birth to me did not make her a mother, placing me for adoption didn't make her less of one. She gave me life, and for that, I will always love her.

I was reeling from the abject finality of it. I had never perceived her death as a possibility in all the scenarios that played through my head. I could tell my dad was saddened by the news for perhaps his own reasons, yet he was heartbroken for me.

I hung up the phone, then quickly found my journals and turned back to my earliest entries. I distinctly remembered when

The Secret Identity of Chance

faced with which direction I was to go at the onset of this journey, and whether to first search for my mother or father, a strong impression had bubbled up from inside me that said, *"go the way of your father."* Had I looked for my mother first, only to learn that she was dead, that would have been the end of my search. I was convinced, more now than ever, that it was the "still, small voice" leading me to my father from the very beginning.

If someone had handed me the mailing address of my biological uncle on my mother's side a few months ago and said, "I think you should reach out," it would have taken me a good long while to muster up the courage to send a letter (and that's on the off-chance that I'd even consider it to begin with). A lot had changed since I'd found my father, and without hesitation, I sat down and wrote a letter to my mother's brother, attached a Christmas card photo, and put it in the mail. I didn't question myself or think twice about it. I was heartbroken that my mother was gone, but all I could do was wait and hope that her brother, my uncle, responded to my letter.

The news of my mother's death left me with such sadness about her life and questions for which there were no answers. Any dreams I'd had about finding her were shattered. The finality of it was hard to accept, but in spite of that, it had filled me with gratitude for the amazing gift of finding my father. Although I hadn't met the rest of the family on my father's side, much to my surprise, many, upon finding out about me, had graciously reached out. I was overwhelmed by the love and inclusion they extended to an "outsider" coming into the fold. I received a beautiful letter from a dear cousin who had experienced growing up with my dad, and her tender words fell on a grateful heart.

Dear Marla,

Thank you so much for the card and lovely photos! I love the ones where Uncle John is leading the girls around

Chapter 11: Chance of a Lifetime

on Vito. He is so thrilled to be your dad and their grand-father. What a gift, Marla, that you all found each other! I have never seen my uncle so happy, ever. It's almost as though something in him was, I don't know . . . kind of un-settled? Instinctively knowing all his life something (some-body) was missing?

I guess what I'm trying to say is: You are the best thing anyone could have imagined—for him, and for all of us. It still boggles my mind—a lot. First, that you were out there, growing up in some kind of parallel life . . . Second, that you found John (and, by default, the rest of us! Oh well, dear Marla, you just have to take the bad with the good!) . . . And third, that we're just instantly family.

Love, Mary

Not All Surprises Are Good

I received an unexpected knock at my door, and it was my best friend, Gingie. I assumed she wanted to hear all about my trip in person and had surprised me by stopping by. I was thrilled to see her, but I couldn't help but notice she was looking very thin. The chemo had left her now completely bald under the blue bandana that matched her powder-blue eyes. I threw my arms around her, relishing one of her infamous bearhugs. You'd never get a fake hug from Gingie. I examined her face, noticing something disconcerting, but she brushed it off, and over a cold glass of sweet tea, she asked me to walk her through every detail of my recent trip. I recapped the moment I'd met my dad, and as she started to cry, I started to cry. She, more than anyone else, knew the aching and longing of my heart, the secret hope I'd carried all my life of someday finding my birth parents. For decades, we had shared every joy and every sorrow.

The Secret Identity of Chance

Once I answered the plethora of eager questions she was firing at me, I again noticed something troubling in her big blue eyes. I finally said, "Okay, spill it. What's wrong, Gingie?"

There was a long pause, and then she put her head down, gently took my hand in hers, and said, "Marla Sue, I didn't want to tell you this before you left to meet your dad. I wanted to wait until you got home. The treatments, clinical trials, and chemo aren't working. My cancer diagnosis is terminal. I don't know how long I have, but it won't be terribly long. I don't want you to worry about me. It's going to be okay, and you're going to be okay. Your father is now going to be the strong lion in your life."

Okay!? In what far-reaching universe was this *okay?* No. No. No! *This can't happen!* Remembering how I had lost my sister very young after a gruesome battle with ovarian cancer, Ginger was the closest thing I had to a sister. The clinical trials were helping; the chemo was supposed to put the cancer in remission. What had happened? I couldn't accept this. I retreated to a place of complete denial. I didn't have the strength to accept the cruel reality of this. I wouldn't. I reached over and tightly wrapped my arms around her while we sat together in piercing silence, and simply cried. Lingering despair had followed me around like a dark cloud for weeks. I could not get my head around the possibility of a life without my Gingie—I just couldn't accept it. It seemed impossible, implacable, and fictitious. I could never "say good-bye" to my rock, my soul-sister, my trusted companion and dearest friend. I needed a miracle.

Emotionally hungover from the news of my mother's death against the backdrop of a terminal cancer report, and all on the heels of such an uplifting and joyous reunion with my father, I was left bewildered and numb. Sorting through the pile of mail I'd just brought into the house and tossed onto the kitchen counter, I saw a strange letter with a return address from Sacramento. It was from my biological uncle. It was a typed letter that included

Chapter 11: Chance of a Lifetime

three pages of copied black-and-white photos of my mother and their immediate family, all carefully labeled and identified for me.

Dear Marla,

I was pleasantly, though not totally, surprised by your letter. A short time before Shirlee passed away, she confided in me that she had given birth to a daughter. That's all she told me. I could tell that she was quite uncomfortable with her admission, so I didn't ask for details.. . she never offered . . . nor did I ever share it with anyone except my wife, Gail. I assumed that because of the time that had passed, and that, as far as I know, she had not told anyone else in the family, it was too painful for her, and she preferred to keep it to herself. I believe it was the hidden heartbreak of her life. Why she decided to tell me . . . I'm not sure.

Shirlee and I were very close growing up . . . and most of our lives. I don't know what you know about the family, but I would be glad to go into more details if you wish. Your family tree has some interesting roots. Sorry I'm not familiar with your dad or his family.

If Shirlee had any faults, it was that she was too generous and caring. Her inability to say "no" got her into a variety of positions that she needed help getting out of. So, she would usually call me. I didn't mind helping her when I could . . . but sometimes I could not. She was like a magnet to those who were down on their luck, and she would get herself into the craziest situations trying to help everyone. Her heart was in the right place, it was just too big for her body.

She was also a very beautiful woman. As soon as I saw your picture, and then the pictures of your daughters, I could see that, fortunately, her beauty has been passed on.

Thank you so much for sending them. As far as pictures of your mother, when my wife passed away, I boxed up most of my photos and put them in storage. I couldn't take looking at them. I am, however, sending you a couple that I did find at home. You're welcome to them, and I'll see what else I can find.

You may want to contact my (and Shirlee's) brother, Steve, and his wife, Carol. They are great people, and I'm sure they would be happy to hear from you.

Love, Ken

His words penetrated my searching heart and gave some context to the mysterious woman who had given life to me. Clearly, there were definite similarities between my mother and me. Although I don't tend to get myself in many crazy situations, I am notorious for attracting those in need (whether they be people, or animals).

Revealed within the photos was not only my mother's beauty (and my inherited green eyes), but a sadness hidden behind her smile. The harsh reality was that I would never get to meet her, hold her hand, kiss her cheek, or look her in the eyes and say, "Thank you."

In the spirit of my newfound courage, I sent off another letter to my mother's other brother, Steve, in hopes that it would also be well received. I was left to piece together my origins and ancestry from my mother's side from whatever family members were open and willing to let me in under such surprising and unconventional circumstances.

What I learned in real time was that sometimes joy and sorrow run hand in hand.

Chapter 12

Not a Chance in Hell

Much to my surprise, I received a letter back from my mother's brother, Steve, within a week's time. It was a lengthy, "typed" letter, with multiple pages of vintage family photographs. His letter gave me lively insight into my mother's Irish family history, along with a meticulous family tree outlining every relative, both living and deceased. I was relieved to receive such a congenial and enthusiastic response. Of course, he was utterly shocked to receive my letter, but he was extremely grateful to know his brother, Ken, had forwarded his information on to me. He confirmed that nobody else in the family had any idea of my existence. However, I'd learned that my mother had been extremely close to her mother (my maternal grandmother), Hattie, all her life. My guess is that my grandmother Hattie was the only other living person who had known anything about me. It dawned on me that Hattie must have been the "older woman" who had accompanied my mother on her trek to Southern California to park in front of my house every year on my birthday when I was a child. In the mix of all the lovely photos and fascinating family history, Steve interjected a touching story about my mother, allowing me a glimpse into who she was as a young girl:

> *Shirlee Ann came from a large, busy, noisy, proud Irish family. She was the beloved baby of the bunch, and she was adored by our parents and my other siblings. We lived in a nice house on Sophia Street in South Sacramento. Shirlee was a very beautiful and outgoing person,*

The Secret Identity of Chance

always willing to help a friend—or to pull a prank if possible . . . she loved to laugh, and she was never at a loss to think up something fun to do. In her teens, she got a job at "Marie's" . . . a little soda and milkshake shop at the corner of Broadway and 14th Avenue in Sacramento. She saved every penny she made (a whopping $300.00), and with the help of the family, she purchased an old green Mercury Coup—what fun she had in that car! She was sixteen and owned the world. There wasn't a "drive-in" in a 20-mile radius that she didn't haunt with her best friend, Lyla. They spent every possible minute in that car.

Alongside the paragraph outlining this story was a photograph of my mother, beautifully posed and standing proudly up against her old green Mercury Coup, with a perfectly coiffed blond bouffant and black-and-white polka-dot dress. I looked surprisingly like her at sixteen . . . minus the bouffant, of course. I poured over each photograph, staring intensely at every picture, trying to imagine her voice, or what she must have been like, or the resonant sound of her laughter. Sadly, these photographs would be all I ever had of her, but I was immensely thankful that her family had openly embraced my unusual arrival and extended such grace to me. I couldn't think of a more meaningful way to honor my mother's memory than to pass along her legacy to her granddaughters.

Death leaves a heartache that no one can heal, but love leaves a memory that no one can steal.

—From a headstone in Ireland

While growing up, I longed for an emotionally available parent I could go to for advice or counsel, and now I'd come to deeply respect and rely on the wisdom with which my father offered

Chapter 12: Not a Chance in Hell

his paternal advice. I was so grateful for our nightly phone calls, during which I gleaned wisdom from his life experiences as he talked me through some of the most challenging and confusing things happening in my life at that time.

My mind felt tormented by the words *terminal cancer*. In the months that followed, the disease had begun to steal away the able-bodied girl I knew. Gingie's robust personality dimmed as she became frail, and eventually completely bedridden. She came in and out of consciousness, while her voice was reduced to a whisper. Her feeble state made our visits excruciating, but I felt a twinge of relief each time a huge smile came over her face when she saw me walk into the room. I did most of the talking, retelling recent stories regarding the amusing antics of my little girls. She would softly nod her head and laugh.

Fortunately, we shared a faith that allowed us the grace of believing this was not the end, that we would be together again. However, the gut-wrenching knowledge that I would have to say a final good-bye to my "Lion of Judah" left me unable to catch a breath. Each time I left her bedside, I prayed it wouldn't be the last. I could not fathom my life without her. She'd always been the strong and fearless one in this duo.

The dreaded day eventually arrived when I received the phone call that I needed to come as soon as possible. I walked into her bedroom where she lay in a hospital bed that had been set up for her in the corner of the room. Her bed was covered in a beautiful, multicolored quilt her grandmother had made. The room smelled of lavender, and the curtains were drawn. Her skin yellowed, she lay very still. Her eyes opened wide, and she smiled when she saw me walk in. I sat down by her bedside and gently took her fragile hand in mine, only this time I left out the funny anecdotes. I poured my heart out, saying all the important things I desperately needed her to know as tears rolled down her hollowed face, and she clutched my hand with all her strength. My soul felt crushed under the weight of words that organically began to form around, "good-bye," but I couldn't do it—I couldn't say it. I slowly stood up, leaned over her emaciated body, and kissed her beautiful bald head. I looked fiercely into her big blue eyes one last time, and like a prayer, I softly spoke the final words I would ever say to her in this life: "I love you, and you will live in my heart for always, Gingie. You will forever be the sister of my soul, in this life, and the next. I'll see you tomorrow."

I walked around in a daze for weeks thereafter. Dozens of times I instinctively grabbed the phone and dialed her number, and each time the shocking reminder of her absence slammed against my broken heart like a two-ton mallet. I missed her robust laughter and bone-crushing hugs. The day she died, I called her cell phone and recorded her outgoing message. I never wanted to forget the sound of her voice.

With Gingie gone, I turned to my father. He had a unique way of helping me untangle the muddled thoughts in my head and revealing reflections of myself I'd never seen. Out of nowhere he would often say, "You're much stronger than you think you are, darlin'," and although I'd been told that before, I'd never believed it to be true.

A Tandem Transfer of Strength

Tahoe and Yosemite were the favored vacation spots in which we had spent countless hours of vacation time together. My father grew up in these familiar stomping grounds, and he knew the scenic terrain like the back of his hand.

On this particular trip, we stayed at Meeks Bay, which leads right into the beautiful crystal-blue depths of Lake Tahoe. The vintage beach cabins located on the sheltered west-shore bay beach are still owned and operated by the local Washoe Indian tribe—an absolute favorite spot of my father as much for the breathtaking

Chapter 12: Not a Chance in Hell

landscapes as for the indigenous people who managed property there. He had quite a few sentimental possessions, but none more endearing than his beautiful, hand-carved canoe. This stunning wooden outrigger was his pride and joy, and he was anxious to show me how to "properly" tandem a canoe. There's something unique and special about Lake Tahoe, with its six different species of fragrant, woodsy pine; the crisp, fresh mountain air, and the majestic mountain caps surrounded by sparkling blue waters as far as the eye can see. The openness of the Sierra Woods brings an immediate calm to my spirit. My dad and Katherine arrived before we did, and as always, he was waiting for us out in front when we finally pulled up in the late morning.

I grew up near the ocean and on sailboats, and I understood it took a lot of work to maintain a watercraft, and masterful skill was required for successful sailing. I've always had a love affair with the water, and the mere thought of canoeing with my dad on Tahoe Blue left me with goose bumps. Soon after I stepped out of the car, he eagerly said, "Hon, tomorrow morning I want you up early, five a.m., so we can head out and catch the sunrise." Our frigid, predawn adventure started with hot coffee out on the redwood deck overlooking the jaw-dropping beauty of the bay. Lake Tahoe in the morning looked like smooth, polished glass. Not a ripple on the water's surface . . . not a sound. We carried the canoe on our shoulders down to the water, then carefully slid it into the cold, pristine water. I learned the hard way there was a right and a wrong way to climb into a canoe so you didn't end up "in the drink" . . . as my dad would say. Lesson learned. My father sat securely stationed at the bow of the canoe, and I sat in the back. We silently glided through the glassy waters, with the chilly morning air penetrating through my less-than-adequate windbreaker. My father and I never spoke an audible word, as both our oars hit the water in perfect rhythm and sync. The surrounding beauty was so magnificent it felt otherworldly, like we were

The Secret Identity of Chance

in a sacred space, one that demanded silence, as if secular voices would defile it somehow. I mirrored my dad's every move as I resolutely followed his lead, trying to keep in perfect time with his pace, adjusting my oars in quick response to his movements as he maneuvered on a dime without any warning. We entered a unique, interconnected partnership in tandem. My father had skillfully navigated us through the cool lapis waters to a point in the lake where we would experience the perfect unobstructed view. With the shoreline barely in sight, he just stopped, and within seconds, a colossal burst of golden light hit the massive body of water and ignited an awe-inspiring kaleidoscope of rainbow colors. We sat perfectly still, mesmerized by the rising fireball of light. Together, we repeated this sacred ritual every morning. I sensed there was an important lesson he was trying to teach me—to trust my own instincts as I followed his lead. Silenced by the majesty of creation, in tandem with my father, he introduced me to my own intuitive nature.

Ask the right questions, and the answers will always reveal themselves.

—Oprah Winfrey

I spent several weeks planning a springtime "butterfly" birthday party in honor of my daughter who was turning four years old. The theme was chosen around her fascination with butterflies . . . or as she referred to them, "butta-beez." My father and Katherine planned on driving down and staying with us over her birthday (as they did for most holidays). If you would have told me when my daughter was born that she would be celebrating her fourth birthday with her biological grandfather, I would have thought you'd lost your mind. As the big day arrived (with everything from butterfly wings for the children, to a bubble machine with pink butterfly nets, a butterfly pinata, and a beautiful homemade

Chapter 12: Not a Chance in Hell

butterfly birthday cake), the very last gift my daughter opened that day was from my dad. She squealed with excitement as she pulled the brightly colored wrapping paper from around the most intricately designed, beautifully ornate, handcrafted butterfly kite I'd ever laid eyes on. It was custom-made of brilliant-colored fabrics from an artisan in the town where my father lived. He was thrilled to give this gorgeous, sentimental treasure to his granddaughter, and that kite was her very favorite gift that year.

Outwardly, one would have never guessed how deeply sentimental my father was, and it often surprised me. I've always found joy in trying to find the perfect gift, and being a good gift-giver means you have to pay attention. Perhaps this trait was inherent, but either way, it was clear we were both learners of people.

After everyone had gone home and the girls were fast asleep, my dad and I headed out to the backyard to sit by the fire and relax after a fun and exhausting day. I could barely see the giant trees in the background of the darkened night, but I could hear the swishing and rustling of the pine branches in the evening's gentle breeze. A warm glow was coming from the roaring fire as puffs of gray smoke billowed up into the night sky. His face was incandescent from reflections of the firelight, but his steely-blue eyes seemed strangely intense. His countenance was heavy; there was something weighty on his mind. After a long, awkward silence, and out of nowhere, he asked me, "Hon, are you happy . . . in your marriage, I mean?"

I was shocked by the question. He had been around us long enough to see the cracks. I replied, "Well, I love my husband. I only wish he wasn't away from home so much. It's hard on the girls now that they are getting older, and he is missing out on so much of their lives . . . and yes, it's lonely for me as well."

He took a deep breath, leaned way back in his chair, and paused while the uneasiness just lingered in the air. Then he said, "Time is something we never get back. Keep your eyes wide open, darlin'."

I felt vulnerable and exposed. I could hear the deep concern in his voice. Over the last several years, family and friends had often shared their misgivings over my husband's work-life balance, and his continual absences. The changes in his personality were worrisome, but all I could offer was excuses ... and not ones even I could believe anymore. The next morning, after breakfast, Dad and Katherine packed up and got ready to head home. I felt the lump in my throat growing as I saw his bags sitting at the bottom of the stairs, and even though I told myself I wasn't going to cry, tears started to flow before I could get the suitcases out the front door. I felt such a sense of safety and security when my father was around. I loved staying up late talking, fascinated, barely knowing hours had passed, when he would say, "Let me tell you another story."

Less than a week after my dad left, the question he'd asked about my marriage haunted me. My once-promising wedded bliss had turned into tumbleweeds of conflict and questioning. After many desperate attempts, I finally convinced my husband to enter marriage counseling with me, which didn't last long. After the very first session, he refused to go back. My father's question continued to ruminate alongside the puzzling words our marriage counselor had said to me as I walked out of his office on the first, and last, day we met. He said, "Marla, I hope everything that is in the darkness will be brought into the light." I left feeling even more bewildered.

"Henny Penny, the Sky Is Falling!"

It was a warm Saturday afternoon, and I was working in the garden when the phone rang. A strange woman with a French accent had called my home. By the look on my husband's face, and a few un-

Chapter 12: Not a Chance in Hell

imaginable questions, my beautiful spring day quickly evaporated into a black, desolate winter. My husband's three-and-a-half-year love affair with the mysterious woman caller was exposed. The cold, dark wings of something evil shadowed over me as I stood frozen in place, paralyzed by disbelief, trying to quiet the screaming voices going off in my head. I remembered what our marriage counselor had said, trying to warn me as I left his office that day, "I hope everything that is in the darkness will be brought into the light." The signs were all there, but in my blind trust and naivete, I couldn't see it.

We were two conflicted, broken, fallible people brought together to make a "perfect marriage," like everyone else. However, the one thing I hung all my hopes and dreams upon was the promise that no matter what happened, for better or for worse, we were in it together, that our marriage vows were something holy and sacred, never to be broken. I lived by these solemn codes, and I'd built a life on the belief that he did as well.

Regrettably, all I could see ahead of me was dismantling the massive ruins of my disintegrated marital union, and the gut-wrenching losses that would inevitably be coming. I stood up and awkwardly backed away, feeling like something violent and bloody had just taken place in what used to be the safety of my own living room, doubting whether my life would ever feel normal again.

I started up the staircase to bed. Step by step, I felt my balance slipping beneath my feet as I grabbed onto the wooden railing to support the depleted shell of my being. I glanced up at the exhausting flight of steps in front of me, realizing that in the morning I would awaken to face a much bigger uphill climb. It would require a strength I didn't possess on my own—and my father's hand.

I'd often thought about the unique timing of my father and me finding each other, and I wondered if this seemingly "coinciden-

The Secret Identity of Chance

tal" joining of our lives together was divinely orchestrated for such a time as this. All I knew was that in the ravages of my once-happy life, if there was ever a time when insurmountable heartbreak left me desperate to stand in the strong shoes of my formidable father ... it was now.

The Last Chance

If you are going through hell, keep going.

—Winston Churchill

I opened my eyes the next morning to silvery light peeking through the cracks in my blinds while strange shadows cast themselves against my bedroom wall. I tossed, turned, and thrashed about during the night in sheets drenched in perspiration, my face burrowed in a tear-stained pillow. The first ten seconds of dawn felt blissfully normal; before my conscious mind was fully awake, and I foolishly thought it was just another ordinary day. At the eleventh second, however, all hell broke loose, and my anxiety-ridden mind began quickly downloading the unimaginable events of the night before. My brain started recalibrating the insane realities of what would now be my "new normal." The emotional heaviness felt like a fifty-pound weight sitting on my chest as I lay in bed staring at the ceiling. Taking short, quick breaths seemed like all I could do short of suffocating. I quickly glanced over at my little girls, curled up together in their matching pink polka-dot pajamas, and a soothing calm washed over me as I remembered all I still had to live for.

These little girls had given me joy that was otherworldly. It was mystifying that even in the midst of so much heartache and pain, love still finds a way in. Perhaps all the years of "single parenting," while my husband was perpetually absent, was really the training

Chapter 12: Not a Chance in Hell

ground I'd needed to prepare me for life as a single mom. Sadly, I can't remember a time when divorce hadn't touched my life.

While my children remained asleep, I tiptoed downstairs, where I quietly closed the office doors behind me and dialed the phone. I was momentarily distracted by the compulsive tapping of my ballpoint pen against the cherrywood desktop—until my father answered. His deep, calming voice wrapped around me like a lifesaving buoy. I said in a whimper, "Daddy . . . I'm in big trouble. He's been having an affair for the last three and a half years."

I nervously waited for his response, and then, bursting out of an awkward silence, he bellowed like a roaring lion in a thunderous growl. Startled, I grabbed the phone before it hit the floor. The only thing my father hated more than dishonesty was a bully. He was far less surprised at this revelation than I was. I had turned my back on my own gut instincts for so long that I couldn't trust them anymore. It struck me that my eroded self-worth had been the culprit in my own demise. I'd heard it said, "We can eventually become who the people closest to us say we are." A decision had been made that I wasn't worth it, and it was easy to believe, given my genesis, because you don't throw away things of value. Years of hiding my heartbreak behind a happy face had cost me something. The concealment of deep despair can be very dangerous—even deadly.

I was in my early twenties when I'd first met Buddy. I accepted a job interview at a high-tech company across town, which I was less than marginally excited about at first. I was inexperienced and primarily interested in working in a fun atmosphere with young people my own age. I predetermined I wasn't going to take the job if the corporate environment was mostly "stuffy suits." The day of my interview, something that seemed all too "accidental" ended up changing the course of my life forever. I parked my car and walked through the parking lot in search of the lobby. There wasn't one large building with a singular entrance, but rather, multiple suite doors were lined up in a row, similar to a strip mall. I just picked a door and walked in. Buddy was the very first person I saw; she worked in the sales and customer-service department, which, much to my surprise, consisted of mostly young people my age. She was a beautiful girl with big brown eyes, hiding behind a flaming-pink mohawk. It was the eighties, and she was the quintessential "material girl, living in a material world," with two-inch-long neon-pink acrylic fingernails and pink bubblegum–colored lipstick. She looked at me, pale as a ghost, and asked, "How in the world did you open that door!?"

Confused and slightly embarrassed, I replied, "Well, I just opened it."

Bewildered, she informed me, "That's a bolted security door with an alarm. It is not accessible from the outside. No one has ever walked through that door before!"

Awkwardly, I slowly backed up and apologized, and eventually found my way to the lobby entrance. The owner of the company ran the organization like a family business, and as it turned out, it was the best company I've ever worked for. The woman who interviewed and hired me that day, and eventually became my boss, is still a dear friend of mine to this day. Coincidently, I met my husband at that same company many years later. The crazy thing was, if that particular door hadn't "mysteriously" opened for me, exposing an entire department full of young people my age, I wouldn't have taken the job. I wouldn't have met Buddy, I wouldn't have met my husband, and I wouldn't have my daughters. *What was the "chance" of that?*

Buddy and I were total opposites. She was loud, boisterous, impetuous, and love-starved, but she brought the fun everywhere she went. She could turn a straw and a dog bowl into a full-fledged party. I was the shy, cautious, amiable one. I had never spoken to her directly until one day when I noticed her crying behind the walls of her cubicle. I watched her for several minutes from across

Chapter 12: Not a Chance in Hell

the noisy salesroom floor. In all the hustle and bustle, people just shuffled on by her, but not one person stopped to ask what was wrong. I nervously tiptoed over to her desk, gently leaned in, and whispered, "Are you okay?" She sank her head low and continued crying. I suggested we step outside, take a break, and go for a little walk. Awkwardly, she agreed, and through her tearful sobs, I learned that her beloved cat had just died. This might seem like a relatively small thing to some, but to a girl like Buddy, it was devastating. She felt like nobody in the world understood her, and that cat was her only source of unconditional love and companionship. In her troubled mind, it was all she had. I understood loss, and I saw the childlike heart behind her harsh façade. From that day on, we were bosom buddies.

We were an odd pair, but we balanced each other out perfectly. She pulled me out of my comfort zone, and I grounded her—well, a little. She later confessed she was afraid of me at first because, according to her, I seemed too "normal," which made me laugh. If she only knew.

Having never had a best friend before, she wanted everyone to know our friendship was unrivaled. She wanted us to have made-up nicknames that we called each other, so we settled on "buddy and buddy," and from that day on, that's what we called each other. We ended up roommates, and we worked alongside each other for almost a decade. We were inseparable. To the outside world, she was often judged as overbearing and lacking in social graces. Behind the façade, she was really a naïve and insecure little girl, desperate to be loved and accepted in elite circles that were not welcoming of someone with her uniqueness. She was terribly misunderstood and taken advantage of, mostly by men. Through the course of our lives, I watched as her neediness eventually frightened most people off, but not me, I was her "buddy." I understood her heart, and I tried to protect her, mostly from herself. I loved her childlike zeal and the fearless way she

The Secret Identity of Chance

chased after her dreams. For years, it was Buddy, Ginger, and me, "the three musketeers," until Buddy eventually moved out of state and got married. Terrible things began happening in her marriage, and after some time, she and her husband moved back to the area. By now, I was married myself, and she and I ended up giving birth to daughters only six months apart. As our girls grew up, they became extremely close, and I loved Buddy's daughter like my own. Tragically, her marriage ended in flames. Her husband started a new life with someone else. The rejection drove her to distraction, and she was never the same.

Although we came to share a common faith, which she said was the only time she had ever experienced real peace, the negative, accusing voices in her head that kept telling her she was unworthy and unlovable were relentless. She consistently rehearsed the agonizing emotional pain of her betrayal, and she ended up in a downward spiral that took days, sometimes weeks, to pull up and out of. I later came to understand that her fragile mental state had probably gone unidentified from childhood, and it skewed much of how she saw the world, and her place in it.

She was gorgeous, smart, ambitious, and loveable. She had a beautiful, healthy daughter, a promising career, and friends and family who loved her. No matter how fiercely I encouraged her to see all the rich possibilities her life still held for her moving forward, the rejection and self- loathing ate away any shred of optimism she might have clung to. What neither I, nor anyone else in her family, knew was that in her despair, her ailing mind secretly gave up all hope. On one November day in 2008, on my kitchen counter lay an envelope addressed to Buddy. It included a stack of photographs from the harvest carnival she and her daughter had attended with my family a few weeks before. I was going to mail it in the morning, but I never got the chance. That night, my phone rang, and it was her devastated mother. "She is gone, Marla." Buddy's finalized divorce papers were in a

Chapter 12: Not a Chance in Hell

sealed manila envelope sitting at her front door. She left a single good-bye letter; it was written to me. She'd quietly disguised her despair so nobody would know she was methodically planning the unthinkable. Who would have known that only a year later, I would be living the same hellish reality in my own marriage. If only she would have held on, we could have locked arms and journeyed our broken road together, hand in hand . . . like we had done hundreds of times before.

My mind wandered back to my own shattered reality while I heard my father's voice echoing his deep concerns for the girls and me. My thoughts scattered like a million marbles hitting the concrete floor at ten thousand feet. My father, on the other hand, was laser-focused.

Uniquely gifted with the ability to untangle very complicated issues, he was methodical and pragmatic, never one to toss out glib antidotes or flowery phrases that belong on a bumper sticker. Although he was intentionally tender and mindfully compassionate with me as his daughter, at his core he was a no-nonsense, matter-of-fact realist. His goal always was to "get to the bottom line," whether that be with people or horses. He said, "Hon, what do you want?"

What did I want? I was conflicted over dueling emotions of raging anger and undying love, both of which felt tormenting. How could these warring responses sanely coexist without destroying me as each demanded surrender to the other? Letting out a deep sigh, he said, "Hon, I want you to listen to me very carefully. You come from a long line of powerful women. You are much stronger than you know. A lot of life is getting back up. No matter what happens, darlin', you gotta remember who you are . . . and you gotta get back up." In the midst of my shame and humiliation, like a protective father, he aimed to restore my inherent dignity and remind me of my worth and value. I recognized this familiar

The Secret Identity of Chance

theme. It echoed the still, small voice, the one that had guided me since I was a little girl.

In the subsequent days and weeks that followed, the madness of unraveling further "discoveries" only worsened. I heard my father's voice as it replayed in my mind while I emptied myself of every last tear and screamed into my pillow until my throat was raw. The words, "you are much stronger than you know," felt foreign to me, like a pair of ill-fitting shoes three sizes too small. I didn't feel strong. It took every ounce of resolve I had to accept such a devastating reality. The man I had once loved had given his heart to another, and it wasn't long before he was back on a plane to France, and I had no other choice than to file for divorce.

She remembered who she was, and the game changed.

—Lalah Delia

One minute I was married, with shared dreams, goals, and future plans. I knew where we were headed as a family. The next minute, I was a single mom, left to cope with the loneliness, stress, and self- doubt of raising a family on my own. Although I was grateful for the love and support of family, loyal friends, and my community, I was still left paralyzed by the scope of difficulties in navigating life on my own. This wasn't the vision I'd had when I married, or the "picture perfect" reflection of what family was supposed to look like. This more resembled the brokenness and dysfunction of my childhood. The irony was shocking.

In the midst of legal issues, less money, and fewer options, I was buried in grief and loss. My saving grace was the love of my little girls, and the nightly phone calls with my dad. He helped me untangle my mental mess, as I began to shadow his strength while mine was finding its own identity.

Chapter 12: Not a Chance in Hell

You can be a mess and still be a good mom. We are allowed to be both.

I chugged down my second cup of black coffee while switching out my third load of laundry. I went over my mental checklist for the week, already feeling overwhelmed. I was juggling life, motherhood, working, bills, and trying to make sure we were on a solid road to healing, and I was doing it all under the umbrella of "creating a happy and secure home" for my children. Alone. Single parenting isn't for the faint of heart. With a husband out of the country, I had been singlehandedly trying to keep all my balls in the air, like so many women left to carry the parental responsibilities of raising children on their own.

Nevertheless, every day I felt a little bit stronger, even on the days when my exhaustion and loneliness crashed into my newfound hope.

Although the days were long, and the future was uncertain, I knew I was growing. Like a seed full of beautiful potential, it must be buried in darkness and isolation before it can take root and come to life. And there were days when I, too, felt like the seeds of all my hopes and dreams had been buried in the dirt. Nevertheless, I fiercely held on to the hope that out of the mire, something beautiful would eventually emerge . . . in due season. Something virtuous would develop in the fertile soil of my current darkness.

Home Sweet Home

We drove up to the house after school one day to see the big, white *FOR SALE* sign firmly planted in the grass of our front yard. It was devastating. My little one sat in her car seat sobbing for thirty minutes in the garage, and she would not get out of the car. Having to move was an excruciating conversation I had gingerly touched upon with them, but seeing the big white sign in our

147

front yard made it all too real. We've had our aunties, uncles, and cousins literally doorsteps away since my youngest was born. My hope was always that my brothers and I would raise our kids together, keeping our close-knit family as cohesive as possible. It's the only home my daughters had ever known or remembered. The sense of security and joy our entire family shared, growing up on the same street, was only multiplied by having all five of our children attend the same school. It was a daily miracle. Selling our family home was part of the collateral damage of divorce, and just another thing I didn't have any control over. The reality of having to leave the only place that felt safe was a devastating loss of unimaginable proportion, but my father gave me clarity and perspective. Home was where our memories were, and they would travel with my girls and me wherever we ended up.

Weekly, I drove myself across town to sit on a cold leather couch with a box of tissues in my lap, trying to unravel the discombobulation in my mind alongside a stranger listening from across a dimly lit room. Somewhere along the way, I permitted myself to be stripped of every dignity and turned into some kind of abstract entity who cooked, cleaned, and raised the children, but who was not respected or treated like a living, breathing individual with a heart and emotions. I was reduced to an inanimate object, like a table or a lamp. Something that could be easily replaced—and I was. My sense of self eventually evaporated.

Sadly, connecting the dots from my childhood and understanding how I had fallen into such a pit wasn't a far reach. However, what I chose to do about it was another matter entirely. It was time for me to learn to trust myself again, and model strength, self-respect, and dignity to my daughters.

My father walked alongside me like a mentor. He helped me understand boundaries and how to better guard myself, and as he put it, "learn to draw a line in the sand." I found new courage and determination. A wondrous spark of hope had begun to emerge

Chapter 12: Not a Chance in Hell

from this dark place as my father's voice played in my head, saying, "Remember who you are, you're stronger than you know." The beautiful thing was, for the first time in my life, I was actually starting to believe it.

You are the North Star in my dark skies. I would lose
my way if your hand slips out of mine.

—Sneha Acharekar

August was right around the corner, and I anxiously awaited my father's call to set up our annual birthday trip. Planning for our shared birthday celebration every year had become an important event on the family calendar. I'd never enjoyed my birthday more. No more wondering if there were parents somewhere in the world who remembered me on that day, or wrestling with unanswered questions about who I was and where I came from. Our shared August birthdays were momentous, and knowing my father would not miss the chance to celebrate with me was an unimaginable gift.

It was early afternoon when I placed a PB&J sandwich and a cold glass of milk down at the kitchen table for each of my little girls. I had turned my back for one split second, and my littlest had covered herself in sticky grape jelly—when the phone rang. It was a Walnut Creek area code, but not a phone number I was familiar with. I juggled the phone while trying to give her a quick cleanup as an unfamiliar male voice began speaking on the other end of the line: "Hello, I am Dr. Armstrong, your father's oncologist. His wife has asked me to place this call because she is unable to. I am sorry to tell you that your father's cancer has taken a very unexpected and mysterious turn, and he is dying. I suggest you fly up immediately if you want to see him alive. I'm terribly sorry."

My mind and body dislodged as I began to scream, "This can't be happening! This can't be happening . . . not my daddy—this

The Secret Identity of Chance

can't be happening!" Terror struck like a lightning bolt, and it spun me out of control. I heard the faint sounds of my concerned little girls calling out to me in the background, "What's wrong, Mommy?" I began lapping around the kitchen island in mindless circles, as if on autopilot. Within the span of a one-minute phone call, everything in my mind and heart had shifted to fear.

I had to get to my father right away, yet the thought of getting on a plane without my children terrified me—especially now. But I had no choice. I'd never left them before, but knowing they'd be with family put my anxious mind at ease. The following morning, I was saying good-bye to my little girls. I hid behind my big, black sunglasses and a forced smile so they wouldn't see my bloodshot eyes and pain-filled expression. I didn't have the heart to tell them their beloved grandpa—their hero—was dying. I simply told them he'd become very sick and I needed to see him right away. With all the other losses we'd experienced, how could I tell them what was really happening? With a looming divorce and an inevitable displacement from our family home, they needed their grandpa more than ever—and I needed my father.

I crammed my body into a window seat, while numbness settled over me like a dense fog. I buckled my seat belt as in my mind the faces of my little girls were all I could see, and I was already desperate to get back home to them. My eyes began to pan over the expansive ocean below. I'd never felt so alone. Large droplets of tears began toppling down my face, my chin, and soon onto my faded blue jeans.

Soaring upward, the morning sun broke through the white, billowy clouds as if the glory of heaven had opened up and the Lord Almighty was within reach. "God . . . where are You? How could You let this happen? Please help me understand."

It was only a year earlier that my father and Katherine had taken a holiday to Peru. My dad was quite proud of the fact that he could still climb to the top of Machu Picchu. I remembered how

Chapter 12: Not a Chance in Hell

he'd brought me back two woolen "Christmas llamas," handmade in one of the small villages they'd visited. I joyfully displayed them alongside my nativity scene at Christmas every year. I think my girls still believe there might have been llamas in the stable in Bethlehem.

My dad knew that his cancer, although in remission, was my biggest fear, so each year he would voluntarily send me his "clean bill of health" from the doctor. The findings always came back the same, and he would say, "See, darlin', nothin' to worry about. I'm not goin' anywhere." I had tucked the last medical report in my purse before I left.

Hi, hon,

The chest X-ray results were all OK. I have mailed a copy to you. See below.

Love, Dad

Dr. Armstrong

Findings

Old, healed rib fractures again noted along the right lateral chest wall. These fractures were identified on a prior chest X-ray. Otherwise, no significant abnormality or interval change.

Pulmonary parenchyma is normal and unremarkable. No evidence of interstitial or airspace disease of any type.

Mediastinal contours normal. No acute cardiac disease suspected. No pleural effusions. Thoracic wall and bony structures are normal.

This had been Dad's last report, just a few months ago, and the words *"no significant abnormalities of any kind"* jumped off the

The Secret Identity of Chance

page. He had been in perfect health—this had literally come out of nowhere!

Blaring rocket engines shot over my head as I exited the plane and made my way to the Arrival section. I stepped off the busy curbside where a family friend was waiting to pick me up and drive me straight to the hospital. I was still in shock, and small talk was awkward and nearly impossible. As we silently drove through the charming little suburban town of Walnut Creek, with its massive tree–lined streets and old, rustic buildings, I almost forgot for a moment why I was there. I felt physical strength draining from my body the closer we got to the hospital. I didn't think I could withstand what was in front of me. "God, please, I can't do this," I prayed, and then I heard my father's voice: "Darlin', you are stronger than you know."

I walked through the white sterile hospital corridor, stepping into the cold steel elevator to make my way to my father's room. As I traveled upward, passing each hospital floor, the anxiety intensified. Like a skydiver going up in the plane, the higher I went, the more frightfully I anticipated the "big jump." As I neared his floor, it felt like hanging off the edge at ten thousand feet, and the countdown began: 3, 2, 1 . . . I froze, unable to breathe, startled by the loud *ding* of the elevator chime. Then the big metal doors opened, and I stepped off into the unknown.

> *The woods are lovely, dark and deep. But I have*
> *promises to keep and miles to go before I sleep.*
>
> —Robert Frost

I stared down at the shiny, white linoleum floor as I walked into my father's private hospital room, trying to gather my thoughts in the few seconds I had, not knowing what I was walking into. There was a large picture window against the back wall next to my father's hospital bed with a view of the business park below.

Chapter 12: Not a Chance in Hell

Sunlight was pouring through the windowpane, filling the room with a warm, golden glow. The blue privacy curtain was pulled halfway around him, and I couldn't see his face—only a brightly colored blanket that lay across the bottom of his bed, one I'm sure he'd purchased somewhere on his many travels. I slowly peeked around the curtain. Our eyes locked, and he broke into a huge smile. I dropped my purse and leaned down to kiss him on the cheek. In his garbled voice and despite his labored breathing, he opened his arms. "You made it, darlin'."

I gently lay my head on his chest so he wouldn't see me cry. Through my cracking voice and uncontrollable tears, I whispered, "I'm here, Daddy."

I heard Katherine's voice as she approached from the hallway, and his eyes lit up the moment she walked in the room. She kissed his head, rearranged his blankets, and gave him some ice chips from a Styrofoam cup sitting on the nightstand. He looked up at her, confused, and muttered, "What the hell happened to me?"

Her eyes welled with tears as she took his hand and said, "I don't know, Boo."

I sat on the wooden chair at the end of his bed observing the tenderness and devotion between them. It was palpable. I couldn't help but think of my own marriage, as the words "until death do us part" ran across my mind like ticker tape. They kept their promises to each other, and the reward was an undying love that endured for a lifetime.

Katherine went home to get some much-needed sleep, and I stayed with my dad for the night. Periodically, he would lift his head, struggling through garbled words, becoming agitated, like he was desperately trying to tell me something important. Leaning in close, I finally made out the strained words he was making a great effort to say: "Get me home!" My father made me promise him I would never let him die in a hospital. He detested hospitals. It would be complicated trying to get everything worked out and

153

The Secret Identity of Chance

hospice in place so quickly, but we were running out of time, and I could see the urgency on his face.

Holding his rough, dry hand, I fixated on the massive bruising caused by the IV plunged into his arm. This mighty oak was falling. I'd never seen my strong, formidable father in such a fragile condition. It was shocking. Finally, he dozed off, and with a pillow and blanket in hand, I fell asleep sitting upright in the padded chair next to his bed.

Sometime just after midnight, I was jarred awake by thunderous groanings. I jumped up to see his arms flailing as he struggled to get free, like a wild animal caught in a trap. "Daddy, what are you doing . . . what's wrong?!" Thrashing about, yowling in agony, he pulled out his IV, but he couldn't speak in coherent sentences. A rush of nurses urgently ran in to sedate him, trying to pry his legs from the inside metal slats of the hospital bed where they'd been lodged. In a fit of rage, he was yelling, but nobody could understand him—nobody but me. I knew exactly what he was doing, and why he was so angry. The noise and chaos finally fell to an awkward silence as he succumbed to the sedation, and the room emptied out. Soon all that could be heard was the slow and steady beeping of the hospital monitors next to his bed.

Still shaken, I leaned in closely and gently took his bristly, unshaven face in my trembling hands. I looked him straight in the eye. "Daddy, I know exactly what you were trying to do. You were trying to break out of here, weren't you?"

His steely-blue eyes pierced straight through me, revealing something I had never seen in my father before: fear. He was like a wild Mustang who'd been trapped, bound, and forced into a "kill pen." To him, the four walls of the hospital room were a cage, and he was fighting with everything he had to get free . . . and make the journey home to die.

154

Chapter 12: Not a Chance in Hell

"Daddy, I promised you—and even if I have to carry you out of this hospital on my bare back, I will get you home! I will not let you die in this place . . . do you understand me?"

He slowly nodded, our eyes firmly fixed, and he took my hand and squeezed it.

I watched him fall asleep, then I pulled back the curtain and gazed up at the full moon against the blackened night. I was losing my Northern Star, and I felt more lost than ever before. My father's bright light was dimming, and he would no longer be able to illuminate my way. I sat in the darkened corner of the room, gazing at the light of the moon while all my beautiful father-daughter dreams began to disappear. One by one, they were swept up and carried off by the whirlwinds of a cruel fate.

As I watched my father lying in his hospital bed laboring to breathe, I knew that now was the time I needed to be strong for him. Whatever befell me once my father was gone was of no consequence. I had to summon the lionhearted courage to face the unimaginable and climb on top of the shoulders of my champion, stepping into my rightful place as the daughter of my strong hero. I couldn't save his life, but I could give him his last dying wish.

Time was quickly slipping away, and there was a barrage of red tape involved in his release from the hospital. It was an overwhelmingly involved protocol with frustrating delays. All the while, the color was draining from his face, and his breathing was increasingly labored. We had hospital personnel working as hard as they could, but the day was wearing on, and I could see the anxiety build in my father's eyes. I looked at him and said, "Remember, Daddy, I promised you." I could hear my determined voice echo in the hallway outside my father's hospital room, urging doctors to move as quickly as possible. He was declining rapidly. It was almost dusk when we finally got the green light. Agonizing relief filled his face as I said, "Okay, Daddy, we're taking you home!" This

The Secret Identity of Chance

moment of elated triumph was immediately followed by the realization of my impending grief.

A young male and female paramedic crew quickly entered the room, asking for my father; they took one look at him and realized time was of the essence. Carefully they slipped a white sheet underneath his backside and rolled him onto a powered cot. He moaned as his face grimaced and twitched at the slightest movement. I briskly walked alongside his gurney, following the exit signs and holding his hand as people rushed back and forth getting out of our way.

The giant glass hospital doors slid wide open and I saw our ambulance waiting out front. I decided to ride alone in the ambulance with my father for the hourlong ride home, and Katherine would drive their vehicle behind us.

The paramedics pushed the gurney into the ambulance and securely strapped Daddy in. I hopped in and sat on a small, padded, fold-down seat right next to him. I buckled the small seat belt around me and grabbed his hand, refusing to let go. I looked around at the intricate medical equipment hanging on the inside ambulance walls and wondered what other heartbreaking stories had unfolded inside this metal frame.

My father gasped in pain each time we hit a pothole or bump in the road, and I would squeeze his hand. "It's going to be okay, Daddy." The young paramedics sitting with us monitoring my father's condition asked one simple question, which took the entire hourlong ride home to fully explain: "Is this your father?"

I began to recount our extraordinary journey and the remarkable father-daughter love story that had been handed to us like a priceless gift—wrapped up in a DNA test with 99 percent accuracy, so there would be no doubt. My father's voice was failing as the pain medication was stealing his ability to speak, and he was drifting in and out of consciousness. He seemed frustrated, as if he was trying desperately to say something to me, but he

Chapter 12: Not a Chance in Hell

just kept squeezing my hand. I got to the part of my story where I found myself going through a divorce, catapulted into single mom-hood with my two little girls.

Suddenly Dad's eyes opened wide, and with a guttural voice, he ferociously forced out the words: "Darlin', remember who you are!" This was my father's last impartation and instruction to me.

As we turned into his neighborhood, I flashed back to that wondrous day when I had turned down Norvell Avenue and saw him for the first time, waiting for me outside his house. Never could I have imagined then that this would be how our story would end. As the beeping sound of the ambulance backing up the driveway signaled that we'd finally arrived, I leaned in and whispered in his ear, "I promised you, Daddy, I would get you home." And I kissed him on the cheek.

He looked up, his steely-blue eyes filled with tears, and said, "You are my good girl." Those were the last audible words he ever spoke to me.

Not a Chance

Above all, be the heroine of your life, not the victim.

— Nora Ephron

I spent multiple days hitting the emotional pause button, trying to put up a brave front, but now my father was gone, and I was headed home. I walked onto the plane wrapped in my dad's favorite leather bomber jacket scented of Old Spice. I staggered down the aisle with mascara running down my face, clutching an embarrassingly large wad of Kleenex, in search of my window seat. I slowly passed by each row as my eyes caught the apprehensive stares of uneasy passengers, each hoping they would not become my unfortunate traveling companion. I finally found my seat at the back of a full fight and settled in.

My father's last instruction to me had been clear and urgent: "Remember who you are!" Those were powerful words. Until I'd found my dad, I had grown up believing foundational things about myself that were never true, and I'd allowed those things to shape my identity. What if this beautiful reunion had been divinely predetermined so that I could tap into a self-identity that was strong and brave, so that I would begin to see myself as a survivor under the shadow of my tenacious father?

Staring out the window into the vast expanse of sky, I allowed my mind to drift off and traipse through the open fields of the *"what ifs."*

What if my father was brought into my life to release a strength and identity that had been within me all along? *What if* this "impartation" was a gift meant to align my heart with a purpose I would have never had the courage to believe without it? *What if,* in a world filled with the orphan-hearted and the brokenhearted, God has chosen a different story for us than the one we tell ourselves?

Chapter 12: Not a Chance in Hell

There's an unexplainable power that's born out of adversity. Something deep within us remains dormant until suffering lays hold of us, and then strength we didn't know we had surfaces. *What if* in the grand scheme of things, our divinely orchestrated lives collided, not only for me to find my true identity . . . but for God to reveal His?

It would take a highly skilled mathematician to calculate the mass probabilities, odds, and ratios of all the events of my life coming together in precise synchronicity, in order to attribute everything that has happened to mere "chance." My guess is the odds would be astronomical at best. But *what if* we are not simply a culmination of molecules simply bumping into one another for no apparent reason? *What if* the highly unexplainable things that happen to us "by accident" are not by accident at all? *What if* the secret identity of chance, unveiled, is actually the tender grace of God?

For most of my life, I had allowed others to tell me who I was, and it cost me something: I faced brokenness, betrayal, and mind-boggling bewilderment as a result. I was walking into a life much like a puzzle with a dozen missing pieces. Ginger was gone, Buddy was gone, and my husband, my marriage, and soon my home would all be gone. Losing my father now seemed impossible to understand. His final words to me battled against my self-doubts as I stared down the barrel of a contentious divorce and faced an unforeseeable future as a single parent. Fear struck every chord in my body, but my father's voice, like a clarion call, began to rise within me. I was about to embark on another uncertain journey, one I would have never chosen for myself.

The Secret Identity of Chance

I pulled out a favorite photograph of my father and me, one I'd kept tucked in my wallet for years. Right behind it was a photo of my daughter holding her newborn baby sister. I held these timeless photos side by side. I saw my father in my girls, and I saw myself in my father. At that moment, the awareness of an impregnable bond that death could not steal took hold of me. My father's legacy would live on through me and my children, and my children's children. His story had become my story, as I hear the gentle whisper of the still, small voice: "I've always been with you."

Printed in the USA
CPSIA information can be obtained
at www.ICGtesting.com
LVHW080902100124
768306LV00040B/228